THE POWER OF ME LEADERSHIP

9 LEADERSHIP TENETS FOR EVERY LEADER

Typesetting and cover design by Arjan van Woensel
Paperback ISBN: 978-0-578-27025-8
e-Book ISBN: 979-888757484-4
First Edition

This book is dedicated to my wife, Kori, who over the years has encouraged, supported, and listened, provided sage advice, and been there for me and our family. Without her, I would not be the man I am today. LD.

THE POWER OF ME LEADERSHIP
9 LEADERSHIP TENETS FOR EVERY LEADER

Leadership potential is within all of us. Yes, everyone can be a leader. In this book, I describe 9 leadership tenets that EVERY leader should embrace and make their own.

The impetus to write this book came from colleagues and students who have appreciated the life lessons I have shared with them over the years. Originally, I intended to write a book of "self-discovery" in order to show people how it is done. Once I read my rough draft, I realized, this: what I have written is simply good leadership that everyone should embrace.

Consider the journey you have taken to get to where you are today. All of the experiences (good and bad) have created the person you are. Most people do not acknowledge the importance of formative experiences when they have them, just like I did not. Once you have completed this book, I challenge you to look within and discover who you are, WHY you are that person, and most importantly, "The Power of Me." It's in there, you just have to identify it and embrace it.

How will these tenets manifest themselves in your world?

All of us can lead.
You can do this.
Good luck.

GRATITUDE

A special thank you to the following who have had a great influence on me: Kordan Kopp, Kaldan Kopp, Geri Brehm, Matt Johnson, Yolanda Johnson, Mike Juech, Frank Eng, and Eric Reinicke.

CONTACT INFORMATION

Interested in booking me for a speaking engagement or working with me as a leadership coach, mentor, or consultant for you and/or your team?
Contact me at: dan@leadingbuffalo.com

BIOGRAPHY

Dan is originally from Platteville, WI. After high school, he entered the United States Army as a military police officer serving in Frankfurt, Germany, The Republic of Panamá, and Fort Devens, MA. Dan served in various leadership roles in the military prior to transitioning into public education where he taught and ultimately held several executive roles.

Dan practices situational leadership while focusing on those he serves.

In 2019, Dan along with two partners started Dinamico, Inc., and works as a compensation expert helping employers make connections with their employees via their compensation systems which helps them attract and retain great people and ultimately saves them time and money.

In 2022 Dan followed his passion and started Leading Like a Buffalo, Inc., and continues to coach and mentor leaders across the country.

TESTIMONIALS

This book is easy to read and busy leaders need great tools like this to help them understand what good leadership is.
—*Stephanie R., Retail Manager*

"We all can lead!" What a great message! I had never thought about the potential to lead that resides in all of us. Even if you have never had official leadership training, you can read *The Power of Me Leadership* and start leading TODAY!
Powerful!
—*Maria T., Director of Business Development*

A wonderful read!
—*Dawn B., Educator*

The 9 tenets are simple, common sense approaches to leadership. Every leader can and should adhere to these tenets. If you don't employ these tenets consistently, you will never reach your leadership potential.
—*Doug R., Founder*

TESTIMONIALS

I love how Dan was able to provide relatable life-lessons about each tenet. It is really easy to see how these tenets will help me in my job.

—*Keesha S., Director of IT*

The way you weave all your experiences (military, educational, other) into the development of these leadership tenets is wonderful. You have a lot of interesting experiences that most don't have. You clearly articulated how these experiences have made you into the leader you are today. Well done!

The 'be the buffalo' tenet is a great analogy/addition to this book. This is very important for young leaders/new leaders/inexperienced leaders. I can tell you that is something I wasn't super strong at 10 years ago when I started and I wish someone would have shared this analogy with me.

—*Ryan H., Public Education Principal*

I was able to take ideas from *The Power of Me Leadership* and implement them at work the next day. I appreciate how the tactics in this book can be used by everyone based on their own situation and individualism.

—*Kordan K., Project Manager*

TESTIMONIALS

There were moments in the manuscript that tugged at my heartstrings and brought tears to my eyes.

As I was writing my notes throughout the work, I must have written down self-reflective five times. As I skimmed over my notes to write this feedback, I highlighted your words which I like even better... a journey of self-discovery!!

Most of what made the book valuable is the fact that you made it personal. The stories, or rather experiences you shared to demonstrate how the tenets of leadership work, made them relatable to me as a leader. You cite real, personal and professional experiences that make it believable as a leader that I can employ these strategies in similar ways in ANY situation and they will likely work!

As a newly retired military leader, the book resonates discipline and commitment to values throughout! I love all of that! I particularly appreciate the fact that from my perspective, our military experiences and leadership skills easily transfer over to our civilian careers, which is a bonus!

Your strategy to implement the tenets of leadership are IMPACTFUL. It is obvious during your tenure as a leader in the military and the educational system, being an INTENTIONAL leader facilitates a sense of COMMUNITY/ TEAMWORK and COLLECTIVISM. All of which makes you an effective leader that builds professional relationships and empowers those around you!

I take pride in believing that I am an effective leader.

This manuscript resonates with me as a leader on so many levels! Many ideals were reinforced and I learned so much as well! You say ' surround yourself with superstars'. I say, you can't fly like an eagle if you walk with ducks. We both get the picture! I would have never likened that analogy to King Arthur's round table, but it works!!

Thank you for this piece of art! I truly enjoyed it and more importantly can take some tidbits away and implement them in my daily work as well empower those around me!

—*Yolanda J., Lieutenant Colonel (RET), United States Army*

CONTENTS

INTRODUCTION

"But I don't know enough!" "But I don't learn from books!" and my favorite: "I don't have anything of value to offer!"

These were my answers to people over the last 16 years, who have said to me "you need to write a book on leadership!" As you can see from this sentence, it has taken me a while to warm up to this idea, but I am finally doing it because I have had some experiences in the last five years that made me realize I do have something to offer.

The main thing I intend to do on subsequent pages is to explain to you my leadership tenets. I'm not going to give you a 12-step process to good leadership. I am not going to cite other leaders. I am not going to attempt to convince you to lead like I do. I am simply going to present ideas on how to improve your leadership through your lens.

Initially, I had no intention of recommending anyone follow the tenets I am going to present to you. My intent was to share with you my journey of self-discovery that may have provided the impetus for you to do likewise. However, now that I have spent countless months writing this book I realize that all of these tenets can and should be adopted by leaders in all situations. No, you will not be able to do things like I do, just like I can't do them like you. But, you can and should adopt these tenets and they will manifest themselves in a manner that is unique to you.

My main reasons for sharing are the following:

1. My leadership tenets may be something you could use.
2. My leadership tenets may provide you with ideas on how to identify and build your own.
3. Seriously? They are the reason I am writing this book!

Now that you understand my intent, I want to enlighten you about my approach to leadership development. Everyone reading this book has leadership skills. Yes, I said EVERYONE. You may not be in an official position of leadership, but you have skills that make you a leader. Here is the trick: identify those skills and make them better. This is what I call "THE POWER OF ME," with the "me" in that sentence being you, the reader.

I currently work with other leaders and focus on The Power of Me in two ways:

1. Coaching/Mentoring leaders by helping them identify their values and strengths and more importantly the "why" behind them. There is power in being yourself and adhering to your values and strengths. We all have them.
2. I help employers look at the power within each

of their employees. I have proprietary software that employers use to create compensation systems that acknowledge and reward the skills, attributes, certifications, degrees, etc., their individual employees possess. This not only helps them attract and retain people who fit their organization, but they also save time and money while doing it!

As you progress through this book, I want you to focus on how the things I describe could manifest themselves in your life. You and I may face identical situations, but we are going to address them differently. That is The Power of Me. You rely on your values and strengths and I will rely on mine. With this model, we both can have success.

Now, a little bit about my background: I was born and raised in Platteville in the southwest corner of Wisconsin, within spitting distance of Dubuque, IA. Unbeknownst to me, we were not the wealthiest of people when I was growing up. My mom was, and still is, a master of squeezing every bit of value out of each penny that came into the home. I grew up in a nuclear family as the youngest of three. I have an older brother and an older sister. Yes, I am the baby of the family.

While in high school I did not apply myself and did not work to my potential. I was that kid who wanted to know what it took to earn an A and once I met those expectations, I would coast. I never thought about leadership, let alone my own, AT ALL! I actually had a coach who told us the captains of the team were going to be firstborn children.

Talk about killing potential! I took his statements to heart and never attempted to lead because I was not the first-born.

As high school progressed, I got bored with school and was searching for answers about the next step when recruitment - educational, athletic, and military in nature - hit me full force at the beginning of my junior year.

It was during this time I was getting inundated with information about post-secondary options that I took my first easy way out (no, this is not one of my leadership tenets and I DO NOT RECOMMEND it). I happened to be talking to an Army recruiter and asked him what would happen to the noise being created by all of the military, academic, and football recruiters if I were to sign up for the Army. He told me it would all go away. My response was something like "you mean to tell me that if I sign a paper indicating I am entering the Army after my senior year I do not have to pay attention to any of these other recruiters?" His answer of "yes" sealed the deal for me and I signed the paper. Once my senior year hit, I also realized that I no longer had to worry about grades. Now don't get me wrong, I did not tank it, but I surely took the easy way out (again). I did not enroll in calculus (I still don't regret that decision, by the way!) Also, I dropped senior English at the end of the first semester so that I could take Creative Foods. I still remember how perplexed my counselor was when I told him I wanted to drop a class in which I was easily earning an A and replace it with my first and only cooking class.

I was just as perplexed when he couldn't understand the magnitude of my new venture. In that class, the students planned meals on Monday and cooked on Tuesday-Friday ALL SEMESTER LONG! Food is my one vice, so why would I not want to take a class in which I could eat 80% of the time?! I look back on those days with Mrs. Robinson as my teacher and relish them.

So, a month after graduation, off I went to Fort McClellan, AL, for both basic training and military police school. Unbeknownst to me at the time, I was starting down the path of becoming who I am.

During my years of service, I was fortunate enough to be stationed with the United States Army in the following locations: Frankfurt, West Germany, Fort Devens, MA, and the Republic of Panamá, and I spent six months in Fort McClellan for two different training stints. I enlisted as a military police officer and rose rapidly through the ranks and finished my career in administrative (army lingo = staff) positions.

Upon ending my tour of service, my wife Kori and I returned to my hometown of Platteville where we both enrolled at the University of Wisconsin - Platteville, with Kori in a counselor education master's program and me in the field biology bachelor's program.

We graduated in 1997 and headed to northern Wisconsin for four years where I took courses at Northland College in Ashland, WI, and earned teaching certifications in Biology, Chemistry, and Broadfield Science, which was just a fancy way of saying I took a variety of classes and I could pretty much teach any science to kids in middle school and 9th grade.

Our oldest, Kordan, was born in 2000 and I spent a year doing the stay-at-home dad thing. Let me tell you, there is not a job in this society that is harder than being a stay-at-home parent. I didn't think I could do anything right, I was always working, and I was TIRED! Props to those of you who have done it longer than I!

In 2001 Kori and I moved "south" to Beaver Dam, WI where I taught 9th-grade science and she was a school counselor in a nearby district. During the subsequent five years we had our second child, Kaldan, and then moved for my job and we have been doing that since.

People marvel when I tell them Kori and I have been married 33 years and have lived in 15 different places. I am just now starting to realize the incredulous response that I get is due to wonderment about how Kori has put up with me for so long, rather than how many times we have moved!

In the intervening years, I have had a lot of conversations with other leaders about personal philosophies and values. When I engage with those I coach and mentor I always go through a values exercise and we discuss how individual values are never wrong: they simply make one leader different from another. These conversations are usually rather easy: most adults are pretty confident in stating who they are and what makes them tick. However, when I ask this simple follow-up question I cause all sorts of grief: "Why are those values important to you?" In other words, WHY are you the person you are? As already stated, most adults can articulate who they are. Conversely, most adults cannot articulate why they are that person.

Figuring out why you are you is not easy.

I had an interesting discussion about why I am me in 2013 when I was getting certified as a leadership coach. I had two esteemed professors who tag-teamed the certification program and let me tell you, it was impactful. At the end of one session, one of the professors was talking about who adults are at their core and she posited that all of us in that room were who we were due to experiences we had by the age of 13.

That comment was right at the end of the session which did not allow time for further discussion. I was perplexed. You see, by that time I had already started down the road of figuring out why I am me and none of the things I had discovered to that point happened to me before age 18. Reflecting allowed me to see that I was one person as a kid and changed once I became an adult and had experiences that provided me with life lessons.

I waited patiently throughout the next seven days so that I could go back to class and challenge the edict made by the professor. Once class started I challenged the comment and stated emphatically that the "why" behind my adult actions was learned as an adult and that the comment made the week before was not accurate if it was meant for all of us.

The other professor immediately chimed in and echoed my response. She then claimed that through her journey of self-discovery she had also determined the why behind her actions and they all occurred when she was an adult. A discussion then ensued and the rest of the participants agreed their "whys" were based on early life experiences. The professor and I were the only two who became who we are because of adult experiences.

Over the years, I processed my leadership tenets and discovered the why behind most of them. As I was doing this I came to realize that I find it very difficult to learn from good leaders. Don't get me wrong, I saw good leadership both in the army and in education, but trying to emulate what I experienced as a follower never seemed to work. Having said that, I was able to learn a lot from bad leaders.

Most of you who have kids can relate to learning from others' mistakes. Before having kids, I never claimed I would be a good parent and I am not sure I knew what being a good parent meant. However, it was obvious to me when I ran into bad parenting. It was almost as if I made a mental note something like: "I still don't know how to be a parent, but I'll never do THAT!" Bad leadership had the same effect on me. I learned to avoid pitfalls that I saw other leaders hit.

As I was pondering this quandary I also lived by the idea that I cannot lead like others, just like others cannot lead like me. I knew things like upbringing, homelife, life experiences, age, gender, ethnicity, etc., create individuals. Thus, uniqueness within individuals leads to uniqueness within leaders.

Oddly enough, I never put those ideas together until 2017 when I was a guest presenter in a high school leadership class. When I was going over my notes before the class I came across those two comments that were listed as talking points. Once I saw them in black and white, I had an epiphany: they are related! I could never learn from good leaders because I am not that person. What works for one leader will not work for another. However, bad leadership is bad leadership. Everyone, despite their individualism, can opt not to employ bad tactics. Learning good leadership is hard. Learning bad leadership that should be avoided is pretty easy.

Now back to the two professors who were in my leadership coaching certification program. One of them helped me down the path of self-discovery by suggesting I determine my enneagram and referred me to one particular book to accomplish the task: The Essential Enneagram (2009) by David Daniels and Virginia Price. I had never heard of an enneagram, but her brief description intrigued me.

Prior to that recommendation, I had taken various personality tests and they were "fun," but not of much value to me. I liked how each one seemed to give a ballpark description of who I was at my core without really hitting a bullseye. Each time I took one, I enjoyed it, but once the exercise was done, I left the results behind and never thought about them again.

Enneagrams resonated with me. I embarked on the journey utilizing The Essential Enneagram, which is an "easy read." No, not like the "easy reads" my college professors over the years assigned, which were typically 100-200 pages full of a bunch of words I didn't know and topics about which I did not care. This book is an easy read because you only need to focus on the portion of the book that is about your specific enneagram.

The process in the book is pretty simple. Read nine descriptors of each enneagram (each one was about ½ a page long) and determine which three describe you. The paragraphs are not in numerical order, so you cannot "cheat" by thinking "I want to be a #2, so I am going to pick the second paragraph." Once you identify the three, you are to go to the latter sections of the book and compare and contrast each one so that you could narrow your choices down to the one enneagram that best describes you.

Well, when I did this, it was a little unnerving. I read several of them and none of them seemed to describe me. I was thinking "Am I broken? There are nine personality types and I do not match any of them!?" Well, I finally got to a section that spoke to me. I thought "Holy &$%#! Someone has been following me around for the last 20 years and wrote this section about me!" The entire thing described me. I finished the task and I could only find the single enneagram that I thought was a match, whereas most people are a mixture of 2-3 enneagrams. I then went to the corresponding section of the book and verified my choice. I am an 8: The Protector.

Once you determine your Enneagram, the book becomes a bit of a self-help tool for each Enneagram. Within each part, there are different sections, and the one that impacted me the most was the "Personal Development" section because of one specific statement: it encouraged me to notice "my intensity and its impact on others." This caused me to understand things more clearly. For years I was aware of how my presence seemed to affect people. I have seen this in other leaders as well. Without saying anything, I can tell when another leader is in the room. It is not position or title, but rather a vibe that leaders exude. Now that I am aware of this as a "self-help" tool, I consciously attempt to control my effect on others when I simply want to exist in an environment.

One other very important thing occurred in my life that has allowed me to understand myself. Before the experience, I am about to describe, I do not think I allowed myself to feel sympathy, empathy, or sadness; you know all the emotions you get when you think of "the feels."

During the time I was working as a principal I happened to catch an episode of Oprah. I am aware of the fact that some of you just judged me for this statement: get over it. Anyway, this episode was about a school program that promoted self-awareness, social awareness, empathy, and the acceptance and appreciation of others and it is called Challenge Day. As I type this, it feels like I am about to embark on an infomercial in which I try to convince educators to bring Challenge Day into their schools. Disclaimer: I am not employed by Challenge Day and will not get any commission for any referrals.

Now back to the story. The focus of that particular episode of Oprah was Challenge Day and its effects on a school in Alabama. I was intrigued and paid more attention than normal. At the end of a day-long Challenge Day program, there is an "open mic" where participants can bare their souls, make amends with others, encourage change, apologize to those they may have wronged, etc.

What I saw in that episode stuck with me: I focused on the actions of two large young men who appeared to be football teammates because they were both wearing high school football jerseys. The discussion made it clear that there were some negative feelings between the two due to race: one was black and one was white. I do not know who apologized to whom, but I do remember them hugging all up on each other and crying. I immediately thought "If Challenge Day can break down racial barriers in ALABAMA, it must be the real deal!" I decided right then I needed to bring it to my school.

Fortunately, prior to this I had hired some excellent educators and they embraced my idea and brought to fruition my goal of hosting Challenge Day for our school community. Challenge Day is set up for 100 kids and 25 adult community members (educators, support staff, board members, clergy, law enforcement, etc), to work with two adult leaders from Challenge Day for 6-7 hours to learn the things I mentioned above.

I have to be honest, I was apprehensive as all get out going into my first Challenge Day. I knew there were going to be feelings shared and I was facing the reality of facing mine for one of the few times in my life.

The Challenge Day experience starts with the adult leaders explaining the logistics of the day and a little bit about themselves and all of them have tear-jerker personal stories that are riveting. Now that I have participated in six or seven sets of Challenge Days I have interacted with 10-15 different adult leaders and I can proclaim that one of the most impressive things about Challenge Day is the quality of the adult leaders they employ. I REVERE them and still have connections with some of them on social media. The leaders are masters at their craft and make Challenge Day come to life.

Going back to my first experience: during the introductory discussion one of the leaders was discussing the participants' comfort zones and stated something like "You probably have a comfort zone that is about a three-foot square." I was thinking "Damn, that is huge! I can't get my size 13 feet into my comfort zone because it is so small!" That occurred about 8:30 am. Fast forward to 3:00 pm and I remember thinking "Where was I when my comfort zone became the size of this gymnasium?!" By that time I had hugged no fewer than 25 kids and 15 adults and bared my soul to four kids who were in my small group.

That evening I remember going home the most exhausted I have ever been in my life. To put this into perspective, by that time in my life, I had already experienced things like two-a-day football practices, baling hay from sun up to well past sunset, and working 36 straight hours as a military police officer. Let me tell you, none of that came close to the exhaustion I felt that day due to the emotional toll Challenge Day took on me.

That next day I walked around school like a zombie. I could only think about others and constantly ran into kids and adults in the building who flashed the American Sign Language symbol for "I love you" to me after having learned it and used it extensively the day before.

Eventually, I retreated to my office and penned an open letter to my coworkers, the board of education, and the community in an attempt to explain the impact Challenge Day had on me. I wish I still had a copy of that letter because I would like to use it as a gauge to see what type of personal growth I have done in the subsequent 14 years. I wasn't sure the depth of the impact Challenge Day had on others until I received feedback on my letter like "Ditto," and "I couldn't have said it better myself."

Brace yourself, this is where it really gets emotional: the following year we hosted Challenge Day again for another 100 kids. We tallied the kids as we ushered them into the gymnasium to ensure we had exactly 100 student participants. Although we had roughly 120 kids return signed permission slips, we ended up with only 99 first-timers.

We needed one more kid and there stood a student who had participated the previous year and he was begging to be allowed in again that year. We let him in.

This young man had made an impact on me the first year by speaking during the open mic portion. He professed to the group that he had no friends and had never been to a friend's house. Now, at the time, this was a quiet, reserved 10th-grade boy who was known by most adults in the school and was friendly and polite at all times. For whatever reason, he had never clicked with his contemporaries and had no friends.

When he made his comment there was an immediate reaction from across the room. One of our male senior leaders, an awesome kid named Steven, jumped up and ran to the kid. They immediately hugged and cried together. They had just become friends.

Now fast forward to the next year when he was a repeat participant. When it was open mic time he again took a turn. He made the following statement that still gives me chills "I would be dead by now if it weren't for Challenge Day." You see, he explained that he had a plan to kill himself the night of Challenge Day the year before, but because he found his first friend that day he did not follow through with his plan.

Wow.

Emotions ran high that day and mine have not quit since. I think I finally realized the magnitude of the impact this situation had on me two years later when I was in front of my coworkers for the last time before moving on to another district. When it was time to say my goodbyes, I became emotional and had to leave the room. Several people came to see me in my office later that day with tears in their eyes and hugged me. I reciprocated and remember telling a few "Damn, Challenge Day," in an attempt to explain away my emotions.

The Challenge Day experience allowed me to look within and helped me to fully understand the things that make me act and speak the way I do.

Good, bad, or in between, I am who I am and I intend on discussing the following topics in this book:

- Tenet #1: Gut Leadership
- Tenet #2: Identify and Address Inequity
- Tenet #3: Lead Like King Arthur
- Tenet #4: Own It!
- Tenet #5: Take Care of Your People
- Tenet #6: Actions Speak Louder Than Words
- Tenet #7: Accountability
- Tenet #8: Be Beyond Reproach
- Tenet #9: Be the Buffalo

GUT LEADERSHIP

Simply stated, Gut Leadership is trusting your instinct. We have all had it and it is very easy to ignore. I would argue it is worth listening to.

In 2006 I landed a high school associate principal job. Interestingly enough I had competing offers for associate principal jobs. Even though there was a $20,000 disparity in offers, I took the job that came with less pay because I "felt it."

What does "felt it" mean? Good question! It is the essence of what trusting your gut is. When I was teaching I had the pleasure of working with a veteran high school principal who gave me sage advice before my first administrative interview and it was something like "You will know the job is for you when you feel it."

Well, by that time in my life I had gone on 15 job interviews and had landed 15 jobs. So, I was thinking "I will feel it when they offer me the job!" Oh, how naive I was! Fast forward a couple of months and there I was facing two offers with a disparity of $20,000 in salary and one I felt and one I did not. I took the one I felt.

How did I "feel it," you ask? Well, when I had my interview, I connected with everyone in the room and specifically the district administrator. After leaving the room a mere 22 minutes after entering it, I thought to myself "I am going to get a call for a second interview!" I was right and then after a second-round interview, I received a job offer in a relatively short period. Unfortunately, the process in the other district was still going on, so I had to ask the district administrator for a week to make a decision.

During that subsequent week, I continued the interview process with the more affluent school district. I had two interviews and met with the principal for a one-on-one tour and chat. As the end of the week approached, so did the deadline for the initial job offer. I made two calls that Friday morning: one to the second district during which I withdrew my name from consideration despite their response of "We will have an offer and a contract to you by the end of the day" and one to the first district in which I said, "Yes, I accept your job offer because I want to work with you."

This was the first time I consciously acknowledged my gut was telling me something.

Unless you have felt "it," the concept is weird. All I can tell you is, just like I have told countless mentees over the years, you will know it when it happens.

Refreshingly, people with whom I have had this discussion have followed up with me and told me despite not understanding me when I first told them, they now understand what "felt it" means because it happened to them. It is not about wanting a job and then getting an offer, but rather it is about clicking with everyone and everything you encounter during an application and interviewing process, which results in the right fit.

Regarding my first time feeling it: I knew that job was for me not only because of the people, but also the overall feel of the school. Simply put, it matched me emotionally. I cannot qualify it other than that, but I am here to tell you, when you feel it, you will know!

Once I started my new role as an associate principal I distinctly remember thinking "I hope I don't suck at this because it is too late to turn back." Well, for the first two months I sure felt like I sucked. I had zero confidence and that little voice in my head kept telling me I was not qualified for the job. It wasn't until one specific incident happened in September (I had started in July) of that first year that I realized I could handle what I was doing.

Early one morning right after the kids were in class my principal and I were walking in the hall and one of our paraprofessionals, who happened to drive a school bus as well, approached us in the hall and asked if we had a moment to talk to her. Due to the fact we were on our way to accomplish a task, I told her we would follow up with her later. We accomplished the task and my principal left the building to attend a morning meeting out of the district.

I tracked the paraprofessional down and asked her how I could be of service. We made some small talk and then she casually informed me she witnessed a drug sale on the bus that morning. Well, I immediately went from relaxed to hyper in about 0.7 seconds. After the initial rush of adrenaline wore off, I relied on my gut to guide me through the situation.

Once I got the particulars from the paraprofessional (just the facts, Ma'am) I began my investigation. By noon that day, I had everything completed, including confessions from the dealer and the buyer. Both were suspended from school pending an expulsion hearing: I did not appreciate drugs and drug sales on my turf.

Just after the noon hour, my principal returned and I informed him why the paraprofessional wanted us that morning. He panicked and went into dictator mode: "Find the suspects!" and "Get some witnesses down here!" immediately came out of his mouth. I respectfully told him to calm down and gave him a full report of the situation.

Principal: "Who did..."   I gave him names.

Principal: "What did..."

I provided him with their written confessions.

Principal: "Where is..."

I handed him the pills.

Principal: "Where are..."

I told them they were suspended from school pending his discussion with the district administrator about their continued enrollment at the school.

I used my former training as a police officer and transferred those skills to a school setting, and let my instincts guide me through the situation despite never having done it before.

Two things come to mind when I ponder this situation:
1. I was able to use past training in a new situation.
2. This may have been the first time my gut led me in the completion of a task: specifically, how to

interact with the kids in question when I was not a police officer and the school-specific logistics I had to navigate. I did not think, I simply acted.

I will address other stories from my tenure in that district throughout the rest of this book, but now I want to get to the essence of what I learned while I was there and that was "trust my gut."

One of the more significant occurrences regarding trusting my gut was based on a fateful hiring decision I made during my final year as a high school principal.

Because my second associate principal was promoted to a principal position after one year as an associate, I had a late opening for another associate. That is when I met Dr. Michael "Mike" Juech, who has been integral to growth in both my personal and professional lives since.

Mike and I immediately hit it off and he quickly became a solid teammate. It was during our first month together that Mike got the nickname that has stuck ever since when one of our co-workers happened to come into the office and ask: "Hey, where's New Guy?" Thus, he is affectionately known as New Guy.

Mike did an excellent job of helping me become a better leader by using one simple tactic: he asked questions incessantly. And yes, I mean incessantly.

For context purposes, you need to know Mike's work history. He worked in a middle school near his hometown and taught literacy and math and had never worked in a high school. Our hiring process was concluded very late that year and he had already started the school year when we hired him. Mike was literally in the middle school classroom one day and was a high school associate principal and athletic director the next. Because all of his teaching experience was at the middle school level, he had a lot of questions. If you are a parent or have been around little kids you know they ask questions ALL OF THE TIME! Mike was like this. (Don't worry, he knows this story.)

Well, at first I ignored the constant barrage of questions. Finally, I started listening to his questions, and the magnitude of what he was asking me sunk in. Instead of "How do you do this?," he was asking things like "Why did you do it that way?," and "How did you know that would work?" He agreed with most of the things I did, but he was seeking to understand the reason I did those things.

At first, this frustrated me, because I could not articulate why I was leading the way I was. After about two months I attempted to start answering his questions. When he asked, "why did you do it that way?" I initially answered something like "Because I knew it would work." He would then ask "But how did you know it would work and where did you learn to do it that way?"

Let me tell you, he hit the mother lode of self-reflecting questions. He forced me to look inside and figure out all of the things that make me tick. Had it not been for Mike, I would not have the career I do and I would not be writing this book. It was he who led me to understand all of the lessons I learned throughout my life and why I act and lead the way I do.

Due to that fateful hiring decision I made in 2010, I started down a path of self-discovery that I did not know I needed.

As I mentioned, I started to think about my leadership

tenets that day and I have not stopped. Up until that point in time, I acted without thinking about the "why" behind my choices. I trusted my gut, made decisions, and moved on. Mike changed that for me.

During this journey of self-discovery, Mike and I stayed in constant contact with one another despite no longer working together. We would speak 1-2 times/week and discuss leadership and various quandaries we faced. Mike has an exceptional habit of presenting solutions when he has a problem to discuss. Most of our conversations about situations in which he found himself usually went something like this:

Mike would start a conversation with "I have this issue and I want to run it by you." Once he gave me the particulars, he would then say something like "Here is how I think I should handle it. What do you think?" We would discuss the pros and cons of his approach and compare it to other approaches he could take. Inevitably, his original idea of how to handle a situation seemed to be the best way.

This continued for about a year until one day when we were discussing another one of his challenges I asked him this: "During all these times that you have discussed leadership quandaries with me and then followed up that discussion with a solution, have you ever been wrong?" He answered "No." I the subsequent discussion I helped him realize that he had an innate set of leadership skills. I told him this was his gut leadership and that he needed to start trusting it.

Mike and I still converse about leadership issues today (we are, after all, close friends and business partners) and he has grown as a leader and has become more confident in his skills. I now rely on him as frequently as he relies on me when we are presented with leadership challenges. We are a good team.

Gut leadership even plays a role when I make a hiring decision. Over the years I have had the honor of being involved in the hiring process of 25 administrators and 100+ educators who would become my teammates while filling various roles within school districts. When I make a hiring decision, it always comes down to my gut: does the person feel right or not?

Near the beginning of my administrative career, I worked in a district where we used an online tool for applicants who were applying for jobs. The tool was comprehensive and allowed the applicants to upload everything relevant to the position in question: resume, work history, letters of recommendation, education, etc. I liked the tool because it allowed me to get an overall feel for the candidates. I never focused on one specific thing, but rather looked at the applicants holistically which allowed me to get a feel for each one.

During a discussion with other leaders about the hiring process, three of us discussed how we evaluated applicants using the online tool I just described. I explained my approach and how it allowed me to get a broad understanding of what the applicants brought to the table. I explained to them how I did not focus on one particular aspect of the applicants' histories. One of the other leaders told me she focused on the answers to the questions that were embedded in the application tool. If she liked those, then the person got placed on her shortlist. The other leader initially focused on the applicants' education, specifically from what institution did these people get their degrees and what their grades were. If he approved of the institution and the applicant received high grades, then they made his shortlist.

That discussion about hiring occurred during the beginning of the hiring season and I consciously thought about it a lot when we were reviewing and interviewing applicants that spring. The three of us involved in that discussion were also the three who determined which applicants were interviewed and which one was eventually hired.

Our first step in this process was to come together and discuss our top ten so that we could pare the list down to about 8 applicants to bring in for interviews. Amazingly, despite our drastically different approaches to how we reviewed applicants (sometimes there were well over 100 for one position), inevitably, we had 7 or 8 in common on our shortlists of 10. Without much discussion, these 7 or 8 ended up being the candidates we brought in for interviews.

My gut feeling is very strong at times. That same spring we had a position open and we received 107 applicants for it. I distinctly remember that number because of the quality of one particular applicant in the applicant pool. After reviewing all 107 applications, I knew who I wanted to hire without even having interviewed anyone because I felt it when I reviewed her application material.

Well, the process proceeded as I described above and we ended up hiring that applicant. To this day I still think this person was the best teacher I ever hired. This educator now works in administration and is doing an exceptional job. My gut feeling was strong enough that I knew by reading the words on an application, who the best person for the job was.

This same thing happened when I was in the process of filling an administrative position years later. I had already met one of our 70+ applicants and was impressed with her enough that I knew she was going to be a finalist for the position we now had open and it would have been a surprise to me had we not hired her. As I reviewed the applicants we had for the position I always found myself comparing the file I was reviewing to the person I had already met. None of them measured up, except one. When I read this one particular applicant's file I distinctly remember thinking "Damn, I am going to have to tell the other person 'no.'" Again, there was no one specific thing that stuck out, but rather it was a feeling I had about the overall application packet that I had reviewed.

Within a week we were interviewing the seven applicants who had made the first round. The candidate who was initially the front runner in my mind was the first one we interviewed and after the interview, I was right back in the "Let's hire this person!" mode because she was the one for us. That feeling was short-lived because we then interviewed the candidate whose applicant materials had wowed me. She blew us away in the interview. I wanted her to start right then and there! I still do not know what it was that caused me to realize this person was the best candidate for the job, but my gut was again correct.

I have also seen other people make decisions based on a feeling during the interview process. Most of the time when I am involved in the hiring process there is a committee of various stakeholders. Inevitably, without seeking to do so, a consensus is usually reached regarding which applicant we should offer the job. During this one particular process, the committee of about 12 people was interviewing our seventh applicant of eight for the day. I definitely "felt" that particular applicant and knew he was the person we were going to hire. Upon the applicant leaving the room, one of the committee members leaned over the table and proclaimed we were done, because he (the applicant) was the one for us. There were immediate nods of approval all around the room. Apparently, the members of the committee also "felt it."

There was one particular time that even though my gut told me one thing, I let the guts of the members of the committee convince me otherwise. Six of us had just spent the afternoon interviewing two finalists for a position. After the second interview, an informal discussion occurred. The essence of the comments was basically, yes to finalist #2 and no way to finalist #1. I was a bit shocked because by this time I had been involved in no fewer than 100 hiring processes and never had the committee not determined a consensus pick. You see, by the time I heard "yes, #2, and no, #1," I had already thought "Definitely #1, but #2 would be acceptable." Despite #2 being my second choice, I went with the collective gut of the committee members and we hired #2. That hire did not sit well with me, but we moved forward.

Less than two weeks later, both applicants had proven my gut right. Believe it or not, the applicant we hired was already showing me some things that caused little red flags to go up in my head. Additionally, the other applicant had landed a job that caused her to have frequent contact with me and she repeatedly reinforced the positive impression I had of her. Fast forward 3 years and the applicant we hired had shown me enough and was no longer employed as my coworker.

Now, referring back to the administrative hire I described a moment ago, I want to address the statement by the committee member. She proclaimed we were done because the applicant "was just like you," with the "you" in that statement referring to me and the rest of my team that was present for the interview. Now, I typically do not consider whether or not someone is like me or not when making a hire. We did end up hiring this particular applicant, and he was a great fit for our team. He fit, but was not "like us," as the committee member professed. I took her comment to mean she felt it as well, and by telling us he was like us, she was indicating he would be a logical, complementary member of our team. She was right.

All of us face a quandary when we hire teammates: hire someone like us, or someone different? Several years ago I was involved in discussions with other administrators about hiring. The topic came up because one of us who was present was about to start his first administrative hiring process. By that time, I had already completed 20+ administrative hires and he was seeking some guidance on how to approach it. He was trying to figure out if he should hire someone like him or someone different than him. He asked me point blank who my best hire was: someone like me or someone not like me. I replied my best hires (I hired Mike Juech twice) were when I hired someone just like me. Immediately, another administrator at the table in a judgy, facetious manner asked "Why, because you had a 'yes man' all the time?" I replied "no" and then paused. My pause was long enough that people started taking their leave and the meeting adjourned.

I stewed on that question and my answer for a month, which was the duration of time between our meetings. I was struggling to come up with a way to articulate why I knew those hires were my best, at the same time I was reminding myself that it was not because I hired a 'yes man.' I was uncomfortable with the lack of depth my answer showed and the flippant comment that it received.

Finally, our next meeting arrived! I started the meeting by reminding them of the ending of our last meeting and I professed how shallow I had felt for the subsequent month due to how I failed to articulate my reasoning for my answer. I asked them to humor me and allow me to answer the question more thoroughly.

I then explained to them the impact Mike had on me and how he allowed me to reach a potential I did not know I had. I explained, as I have done with Mike since then, that because we are wired the same way, it feels like Mike is in my head when we are discussing something. We rarely focus on the how of anything, because we both know the "how." Instead, we focus on the "why." Because of this, I feel like he is in my brain: it is as if I am having a debate with myself, which has really helped me better articulate my reasoning and my actions.

Speaking of "being wired the same way," I do not mean that Mike and I are identical, but rather we view the world in a similar manner. There is one glaringly (at least to me) obvious way we are different: he has better interpersonal communication skills than I do. Mike is sincere, affable, and warm, naturally, whereas I have to work at it. We both can "work a room," but it is natural to him to do it, whereas I have to consciously focus on it.

Now that I have explained my approach to hiring I feel as if I need to clarify something. Hiring someone like me (Mike) would not have made sense if we worked in isolation or we were a team of two. If everyone on a team is the same, I would argue points of view and approaches to issues would be overlooked because of the common line of thought. That would not be healthy for any small team.

It is time to start listening to your gut. Some may call it intuition or a sixth sense. Regardless of how you define it, you should acknowledge it, embrace it, and most importantly, trust it. All of us have unique experiences that cause us to have gut feelings. Start tapping into yours.

IDENTIFY AND ADDRESS INEQUITY

Everywhere you look in society there is inequity. Females get treated differently from males. People of color get treated differently than white people. Inequity permeates every facet of American society.

I have a confession: I was not always outraged by the poor treatment some people received from others based on things like ethnicity, race, sexual orientation, etc., due to ignorance in the true sense of the word: I simply did not know it was an issue. Fortunately, during my enlightenment period of working in public education, I became more aware of the inequities that exist in society.

My thoughts on inequity are not political in nature, but rather human in nature. We must accept others for who they are. Period. Seriously, it is that simple. If someone is different than you, GREAT! Wouldn't the earth be a rather mundane place to live if we were automatons who looked alike, thought alike, and acted alike? I know I am a better me because of the influence of others. Everyone is different from me and thus, I can learn from them.

I did not have aspirations of making new and interesting friends when I joined the army: it was an easy way out of high school and my home town and I jumped at the chance to do it. A month after graduation I found myself in Basic Training and Advanced Individual Training in Fort McClellan, AL. After training, I was still young and impressionable and was stationed in Frankfurt, West Germany, as a proud member of the 109th Military Police Company.

When I first arrived in the 109th, our company's mission was to guard the United States Army's V Corps Headquarters, which was in the Abrams Building on the Abrams Complex in the heart of the city. We were unofficially known as the "palace guards."

During that first duty assignment, I was part of a package platoon: 20 of us started training together in Fort McClellan and 18 (I think) made it successfully to Frankfurt. While in Frankfurt I met a lot of wonderful people, consumed my share, and probably a few other people's share, of fermented beverages, and had a great time, at least when I wasn't working.

One of the people I met while stationed in Frankfurt was a junior non-commissioned officer named Frank Eng. Frank is 7-8 years my senior and was born and raised in Brooklyn, NY, to an African-American mother and a Chinese-American father. Frank is large by most people's standards and I would estimate that he is about 6'5", 250. I am probably underestimating the weight, but he might read this and I want to continue to have him call me his friend.

When we first met, Frank was everything I knew I wasn't: smooth, confident, intelligent, and cool. He had a way with words that allowed you to understand his passion and commitment to those things about which he cared: his family, those he led, and the United States Army. I was immediately drawn to him. At that time I did not dwell a lot on leadership, but I knew I found in Frank someone I could look up to. Unfortunately, I did not seek to take to heart the things he told me; at the time, anyway.

Throughout our time serving together in the 109th, Frank and I became very close. Close enough in fact that he was my official witness when Kori and I got married in the Roemer in Frankfurt. You see, I was required to have a witness due to the official nature of the proceedings and the fact that it was all conducted in German. On a side note, I still wish I had brought someone with me who spoke German! Pardon me, but I digress.

During the various shifts we had together, whether we were patrolling the streets of Frankfurt or playing spades in the military police breakroom of the Abrams building, Frank and I spent a lot of time talking about life before the military. I do not recall what, if anything, I shared with him. I am sure I did, but because they are my stories, I cannot remember to whom I have told them over the years. However, I remember many things he shared with me.

I distinctly remember talking about baseball, specifically the '69 Mets. I was thinking "Dude, I was like 1! You remember the '69 Mets?! How old are you? Damn, you're old!" I guess in those days, "old" was being in your late 20s. Oh, how wrong I was.

Other things he told me were about the old neighborhood in which he grew up: the Bedford Stuyvesant section of Brooklyn, aka Bed-Stuy. I don't recall all of the specifics, but I do remember some of the key points: Frank's world growing up was confined to the limits of his neighborhood. He and his friends were living the life and no one ever got out. He repeatedly focused on how "hard" it was to get out of the city and do something with his life other than perpetuating the only life he knew. I did not understand the magnitude of that statement for years. Frank did get out and spent some time in Iowa playing basketball collegiately.

I cannot tell you whether or not Frank ever boasted of his prowess on the court, but I can tell you about some of his life in Iowa. There were some crimes in the city in which he lived and it only made sense to the local law enforcement authorities that the black guys in town who were there to play basketball must have been involved and should be questioned. I do not remember the particulars of the situation, but I was left with a sense of unease when I encountered this situation in which someone near and dear to my heart had been questioned about a crime just because he had a certain color of skin. I doubt this was the first case of blatant racism I encountered, but I can tell you it was the first time it affected me personally. Even as I write this I have the urge to tell the police in that city in Iowa how wrong they were.

Frank's basketball career ended abruptly because of that incident and I can only assume he would have gone pro had he been able to stay in college; well, at least that is my spin on things! Anyway, once that portion of his life was truncated, he ended up enlisting in the United States Army as a military police officer and that is why our paths crossed in 1987.

Now getting back to his proclamation that it was "hard

to leave the neighborhood:" I get it now. During an equity workshop in which I was involved in 2018, my eyes were opened to the historical inequities that exist in our society. Up until that point I was blind to it and now I often ponder my ignorance.

I think I find it hard to recognize societal inequity for two specific reasons. First of all, I am a middle-class, white male in the United States of America. I am not ashamed of this, but I can admit the fact that society is set up to benefit me. I benefit in tangible and intangible ways every day, therefore, inequity is not something that is at the forefront of my mind most of the time.

Additionally, I was born and raised in Wisconsin and after 8.5 years stationed in various countries around the world, I have been back in Wisconsin for 25+ years. Wisconsin is segregated and mostly WHITE when you get away from the cities. Because it is lily-white Wisconsin that I have called home for 40+ years, racial inequity is not something I encounter every day. To put it more clearly, I benefit from racial inequity and rarely encounter it due to the lack of diversity around me, therefore, it is not present to register in my consciousness. This is problematic for me.

It is the acknowledgment of these inequities that make me finally understand what Frank meant when he made that statement to me back in the 80s. Society, the system, and simply put, everything, was set up against him so the easiest path before him was one that allowed him to perpetuate the life he knew in Bed-Stuy. There was no support system within his community that allowed young men and women to explore other options. Most felt stuck. Now that

I get it, I must continue down the path of allowing myself to see inequity when I encounter it. Doing so makes me an ethical leader. Not doing so is not an option.

As I have mentioned, it is not necessarily easy to identify inequity if you benefit from the situation. People must consciously be aware of situations and consider the ramifications of their actions and ideas.

An example of this occurred in one of the districts in which I worked. In that district, there was a teacher of music who mandated kids participate in all of the concerts that were associated with that course. To ensure compliance with this requirement, there was always a grade associated with attendance and participation in concerts. This makes sense, on the surface, but if you examine it through an equity lens you can see how this is not a good practice.

Please consider kids who come from families/homes that have a low socioeconomic status. Typically, these kids do not have the luxuries that kids in the middle or upper classes have. At times, these kids may be responsible for taking care of siblings in the evening because the parent(s) is working. Additionally, money for gas and/or accessibility to a vehicle may be issues. Now that you consider these factors, it should be plain to see that it is quite possible that a student's home life could prevent him/her from attending and participating in a concert, thus, that student would earn a failing grade for not attending that particular concert. It is examples like these that occur regularly in our society and until we truly think about the situation, it is easy to ignore the inequity that exists.

During the writing of this book, other events have

occurred that must be addressed. On August 23, 2020, Jacob Blake, a 29-year-old black man, was shot several times by a police officer in the city of Kenosha, WI. The shooting was caught on video and caused massive demonstrations and protests by people who support the movement, Black Lives Matter. This struck home for various reasons. First of all, my wife and kids have mixed heritage and are considered to be people of color, despite the fact their skin tones are rather light. Additionally, I live in Kenosha County and I was familiar with the areas in which the shooting and subsequent demonstrations occurred. Because of its proximity, I also had co-workers who lived in Kenosha. The proximity to these events made them more real to me.

Also, that spring and summer Breonna Taylor was killed in Kentucky and George Floyd was killed in Minnesota. These events caused demonstrations and unrest throughout the country and caused me emotional grief when I saw the images of people of all colors and from all walks of life coming together to protest the systematic oppression that exists in our country. Most of us did not create it, but all of us must work to defeat it.

The pain of these events and the inequities hit home when I saw a picture on social media of one of my closest friends, Matt Johnson, a black man originally from Harlem, who was carrying a sign in a protest march that read "Am I next?" The mere thought of that picture haunts me and causes an extreme emotional response to this day.

Now that I am writing this, I am reminded of another equity discussion I had with a leader about 15 years ago. I was in the midst of applying for jobs in new districts and another leader and I were discussing school mascots.

I do not profess to completely understand the depth of oppression that indigenous people feel when faced with racist school mascots, but the fact that they are offended is enough for me to understand there is an issue. Due to this, I have never once considered working for a district that has a racist mascot. I expressed this conviction to my fellow leader and he did not seem to understand. He asked me something like "what would you do if you went to a district that had mascots that were considered racist by some?" I told him I would not apply for jobs in those districts. He was incredulous.

Just like I opted to not get a pupil services director license, a curriculum director license, or a business manager license because I did not want to do those jobs, I refused to apply for jobs in a district that had racist mascots. I know what I want, and more importantly what I don't want, and I stand by those convictions.

Inequity is all around us. It permeates the very fabric of our society. It is easy to be oblivious to inequity if you benefit from it or do not routinely encounter it. I am merely suggesting that it is time to actively seek it out and do everything within your power to rectify it. It is incumbent upon leaders to stand for what is right and just. When we are faced with inequity, we must address it.

LEAD LIKE KING ARTHUR

Most, if not all of you, know the legend of King Arthur and the Knights of the Round Table. He and his trusted advisors routinely met around a round table that allowed them an equal say in the proceedings at hand. I embrace this concept wholeheartedly.

In 2008 I had the honor of being promoted from an associate principal position to a principal position. By that time in my career, I was starting to enjoy the hiring process. It excited me because I saw endless possibilities for some of the candidates we brought in for various positions. Hiring for my replacement was no different.

We had 70+ applicants for the associate principal chair that I was vacating and I was leading the search for the right person to replace me. I remember encountering several names of people I knew from previous work experiences or professional development opportunities I had over the years and I was pleased with the overall depth of the candidate pool.

I distinctly remember the day we did the interviewing: we started at 7:30 am and interviewed people ALL DAY

LONG. With a few meal breaks mixed in, we were done at 8:00 pm that night. I was extremely excited about the quality of the applicants we interviewed and all of them had bright futures in educational leadership. We came to a consensus on two finalists, one of whom was a former coworker. She dazzled us with her intelligence in the interview, and I marveled at the depth of knowledge she displayed.

Once she accepted the job, I remember sitting in my office from 1 pm-2 pm that spring afternoon thinking something like: "@#%$, we just hired someone with skills so great that she is going to make the current associate principal look like an idiot." Yes, I was thinking about how I had just hired a person who had better skills than I, and she was going to make me look bad. I still do not remember how I snapped out of wallowing in self-pity, but I did. It only took me an hour to accept the fact that I was not going to be the best and that I should embrace her superior intelligence.

I had accepted and bought into a concept that all great leaders embrace: surround yourself with superstars.

Fast forward to that fall when I was working with our newly hired associate principal. Because I knew of her intelligence and skillset, the flow of information between the two of us was a two-way street. She had the technical skills and knowledge from her voracious appetite for educational literature and I had my gut telling me how to lead. The two of us made a good team. One specific skill she had was her ability to read something, quickly understand it, and then relate it to other things she already knew, whether it was specific to education or contextual. She was a master of applying new knowledge. As that year progressed I continued to marvel at her knowledge and skillset. We had daily interactions in which I learned from her and she (hopefully) learned from me. She would tell me about new knowledge she linked to already existing knowledge and I helped her grow closer to mastery in leadership. We made a good team because our skillsets complemented each other. After that year, my associate moved on to a director position and my leadership tenet of leading like King Arthur was affirmed.

Most of us know the story of King Arthur, real or not, and his famous Round Table. King Arthur had a myriad of close confidants who we know as his Knights of the Round Table. They were all worthy of praise in their own right and he just happened to be the King. Because of their knowledge and ability, he had deep respect and admiration for them, and when they counseled together, they sat at a round table so they all had a voice in the topics/decisions at hand, even when it was the King's decision to make.

This is how I lead.

My teammates have valuable insights and points of view I need to hear to get better at my job and make better decisions. Thus, I engage with them regarding most of the things that cross my desk. I can only be as good as they allow me to be and we are better together than I am alone.

I have often lamented with my teammates over the years regarding the shapes of the tables at which we have held meetings. It is rare to find a room that can accommodate a round table that seats 8–12 leaders. Therefore, rectangular or oval tables seem to be the standard for conference rooms across the country. Unless I am last to arrive and the "head" of the table is the only seat available, you will not find me sitting there. I prefer the side of the table on the end. This makes me comfortable and allows me to be present in a meeting. I never want to claim the head of the table and have that action be interpreted as a power move. This is not me.

I believe in King Arthur's approach so much that I have an Excalibur tattoo on my back that is about 18" long. Tattoos are personal and I know what the tattoo is and what it means. Others, however, have thought it was a cross, or that I have a dagger stabbing me in my back: both cause me to chuckle.

When I talk about this specific leadership tenet, some people easily grasp the idea of leading as if we are all around the table having an equal voice. However, grasping something and truly understanding something are not always the same.

So that brings me to King Arthur and the tissue box. In 2019 I was in a meeting with CEOs, executive directors, company presidents, and various other executive leaders and our topic was leadership. Two colleagues were discussing a specific leadership quandary that had affected each of them simultaneously in their professional roles. Both of them responded in a manner that they thought was logical. By that time, both of them had put the challenging situation behind them, but neither one professed to have "won" in the situation: it was simply over.

During the discussion, one of them made a statement something like "I did what I normally do and you did what you normally do. Maybe we should have done something halfway in between and we would have had better results."

I let that sit there. And sit there. And sit there. I pondered his statement for quite a while.

Because over the years I have tried to listen more and speak less (a tactic I learned from a former coworker and outstanding leader, Steve Vessey), I consciously did not talk while I was pondering this interaction for the next 90 minutes. Finally, I had an epiphany. During the discussion between those leaders there happened to be a tissue box on the table between them. Its placement made my "Round Table" thoughts more tangible.

In essence, one of them suggested that if they had acted more like King Arthur, whereas, each of them had a voice and their actions were a blend of both ideas, their respective outcomes may have been better.

Now, consider the placement of a tissue box on a conference room table during a meeting: it rarely moves, unless, of course, your meeting is emotional, then who knows where that thing ends up!

Anyway, let's assume the tissue box is the answer that is being sought. If a single member of a team does not talk with others about a decision he/she needs to make, that tissue box will sit right there in the lap of that person who has to figure out the problem. However, if that person were to discuss the situation with others, he/she will most likely encounter new knowledge and/or a point of view that had not previously been considered.

As more people have input on the situation, the tissue box/decision moves around the table. Going into a situation like this, no one knows where the tissue box will end up. It could remain in the lap of the person who is leading the discussion, or it could end up somewhere else on the table. Without that discussion, no one would know what the best decision is.

Another powerful example of how leading like King Arthur involves another one of my coworkers and now partner, Dave Betz. I had just started a new educational leadership position and was meeting with my team. I had already noticed how Dave said little, but when he did speak, his point of view was usually drastically different from other points of view that had already been voiced. It is easy to assume that his point of view was wrong due to it being so different from other ideas that were discussed, however, that was never the case.

Two specific reasons this situation occurred: my predecessor did not lead like King Arthur, but was rather autocratic; plus, Dave was not a trained educator; he was the money man and was rarely, if ever, given a voice. Additionally, it seems as if his ideas were always "outside the box" because they were not developed through an educational lens. Once I recognized the untapped resource I had in Dave, we became a better team and a better institution. Over the years I witnessed Dave gain the confidence he needed to lead. I benefited greatly because of the influence he had on me. I know I am a better person and leader due to the insight he shared then and continues to share with me now.

Leading like King Arthur can be humorous at times. One summer I got on my soapbox with my team and described to them at length the importance of leading by gaining many points of view and discussing things with other leaders. Part of my diatribe entailed acknowledging we had some impressive brainpower and ability when we put our collective minds together. I then stressed the importance of this approach in contentious situations: I convinced them that because of our collective ability we could conquer any problem or situation that came our way. I said, "There is nothing in education worth getting worked up about. When we encounter issues, we will discuss them and figure them out."

That fall during professional development time with the staff, one of the other administrators used this concept and tried to convey the importance of collaboration. He said to them "Just like Mr. Kopp says, there isn't anything in education worth getting excited about."

What? Excited, yes! Worked up, no! I jumped up and made my way to the front of the auditorium. I interrupted and said the following: "What Mr. Kopp said was 'There is nothing in education worth getting worked up about!' Yes, you should be excited! Please just don't get worked up. We will figure it out!" Laughter ensued.

In summary, I would like to remind you that you do not have all the answers. Most likely, you have some very good ones; however, are you positive all of your decisions are the best? Engaging your teammates and leading like King Arthur is something that will help you ensure your decisions are the best they can be. None of us have all the answers, but collectively, we are more apt to have success and ensure proper placement of the tissue box, if we engage one another.

OWN IT!

Own it! In other words, take responsibility. This is huge.

What does it mean? Who is it referencing? Do I need to do it? All of these are good questions and it is just in the last few years that I have consciously begun to piece this one together.

To put it succinctly: accept that you are responsible for your actions, your performance, your emotions, the organization's mission, those you serve...and the list goes on.

Even as I write this, I am a bit perplexed about where the idea of owning it crept into my subconscious. This may be the one leadership trait that I exude that I cannot trace back to its origin.

A time that stands out as a prime example of owning my actions was when I made a poor recommendation to a board about something. I thought I was doing the right thing, but I had misunderstood the background information that had been given to me when I chose the best placement for the tissue box. After the board took action, there was pushback from within the organization. I sought clarity from other leaders so I could understand what went wrong. Once I clearly understood the issue and determined that I had misunderstood their original input, I sent a communication to my coworkers in which I acknowledged and owned my error. This went over well. I showed them that owning it can and should be done at all levels of an organization.

Another specific time I accepted responsibility for my actions endeared me with the board for which I was working at the time. To give you all some context, two or three years before the following discussion we had hired a person who did not work out well and caused some havoc in the organization before leaving. I was having a conversation with members of the board about hiring practices and I informed them we were not perfect because we did not always hire the right people. I mentioned the particular individual and told them I made a mistake when he was hired. Immediately, the board president roared "Oh, no you don't! I was on the committee and ALL of us screwed up. It wasn't just your fault!" I thanked him for his response, but argued a bit and told them that I had led them down the path of hiring this person, thus, it was my fault. He acquiesced and I gained more respect from them because I had owned it.

My first recollection of owning it as an adult occurred when I was working as a military police officer in Fort Devens, MA, in 1991. I was patrolling at the beginning of my shift one crisp fall morning and happened to be rolling through the 15 mph school zone during the morning rush of kids getting dropped off at school. Near one end of the school zone, there was a hill and I was approaching it from the top when an oncoming car crested the hill and approached me going 45 mph. I did a quick u-turn and once I was out of the school zone, easily caught up with the car. Upon affecting the traffic stop, the driver became indignant when I informed him that I had him going 45 in a 15 and that I needed to see his license. He immediately demanded to see my radar.

Now, back in 1991, I was a bit brash. I knew I didn't have him on my radar: I had simply estimated his speed based on my training. At that time, all the members of the Fort Devens Military Police Company were certified to run radar. Part of this certification process entailed being tested by a state trooper and we had to accurately identify speeds without the use of a radar gun. We were tested on a plethora of vehicles and consistently had to be within one mile of the actual speed as determined by a radar gun in the hand of the trooper. This certification even came with a fancy certificate with my name on it! I wish I still had that thing because with that and $4 I am sure I could pretty much go into any coffee shop around here and get a Cafe Americano!

Anyway, I didn't have this guy on my radar, so showing him my radar would have been pointless; not to mention there was no legal requirement to do so. Despite all of that, I told Speed McQueen "yes", and he could see my radar. He immediately unbuckled his seat belt (at least he did that right) and opened his car door. I quickly told him to stop what he was doing and get back into the vehicle and buckle up. As he was complying he told me he was just going to go and see my radar as I told him he could.

Well, this is where the brashness comes in. I told him to look over his right shoulder. He complied. I then told him he could clearly see my radar on the dash of my cruiser right from where he was already sitting; thus, he didn't need to get out of his car. Needless to say, my attempt at humor did not sit well with him. I proceeded to issue him the ticket and we parted ways.

So, you are probably asking something like "what does this have to do with owning it?" Well, I knew what I had done was probably not the ideal approach to law enforcement so I headed back to the station to tell the Desk Sergeant about the situation. I parked behind the station and entered it via the backdoor. The Desk Sergeant was free so I told him what I had done and that I was wrong. I also told him I suspected the guy was going to make a formal complaint and that it may be warranted. I no more than said that and in walked the soldier from the traffic stop to complain.

The Desk Sergeant took the verbal complaint and the soldier left the station. The Desk Sergeant then spun his chair around so that he could again engage with me as I was standing behind the desk beyond a waist-high partition. After a few moments of contemplation, he simply gave me a look and told me not to do it again. His reaction to me owning my idiocy caused me to think about how powerful it was to take ownership of one's behaviors. I am convinced had I not owned it, I would have been in a little bit of trouble, and justifiably so.

I guess now would be an appropriate time to apologize to that soldier, so here goes: "Sorry, Specialist, for being an idiot and now not remembering your name after all these years."

When I was in education I tried to teach the kids how

to own their behavior. In one particular district in which I worked there was a table at lunch that over the years was populated by a group of mostly young men who liked to push the boundary of appropriateness. Well, one day I saw a relatively large piece of pizza fly across the commons like a frisbee and I saw that it had come from that table. I walked over to them with the immediate, obvious response from them and all others near them of "OOOOOOOO!" I asked who did it and one 11th-grade boy immediately told me he did. Everyone else at the table was laughing.

Once I got them all to calm down, I simply told the young man to refrain from yinging pizza like a frisbee in the future. I then got on my proverbial soapbox and pointed out to the rest of them how he had owned his behavior. I tried to make them understand that by immediately owning his behavior, I simply asked him to stop. Had he lied or given me grief, he may have ended up with some type of consequence.

I didn't think much of this incident until the following week when I encountered this same young man with some of his friends in the hall. They were causing a disruption and I asked them what was going on. One of the boys started talking back to me and the pizza yinger immediately piped in and said "own it, dude! Just tell him you did it." The other kid fessed up and I gave them a verbal admonishment and moved on.

Several times throughout the remainder of that year I encountered the same group and inevitably they were acting or speaking inappropriately. It became very routine for them to holler out "own it!" as I approached them.

For those of you who have kids of your own, you know

at times kids grasp the own it concept, at least to some degree. Think of all the times your kids may have done something "bad." Frequently, the offending child will rush to a parent to tell the parent of the mishap before the parent finds out on his or her own. Yes, they are practicing the concept of owning it with a little bit of spin control thrown in for good measure.

Now that I wrote that last part, it made me recall other situations in which I forced "owning it" onto kids. Because I am well aware of how kids can spin stories to reduce their culpability, I used a tactic as an associate principal that still makes me chuckle.

When dealing with disciplinary situations, I would frequently make calls to parents while on speakerphone with the offending kid in my office. Once I identified myself I turned the conversation over to the kid so he/she could tell the parent what he/she had done wrong. Yes, this was forced "owning it," but it also allowed me to ensure there was no spin control going on. I hope that at least some of the kids got some leniency at home because of owning it. Also, unbeknownst to the kids, I used this tactic so the parents could simmer down a bit before the conversation they were going to have at home later that evening.

Another time that I owned it proved to be very powerful. I was interacting with a group of disgruntled coworkers and one of them in a terse manner exclaimed "You always get defensive!" I responded with, "Yes, I do and I shouldn't." This coworker did not know how to respond to me! I had effectively disarmed her by owning the poor behavior that she had pointed out. She was right and I acknowledged it. She immediately calmed down, and we subsequently had an excellent discussion about their concerns. We worked together for a decade and before that interaction, she always exuded an adversarial air of distrust. Once this interaction occurred, she became much more amicable and I began to appreciate her as a coworker.

Yet another time of owning it occurred when I was a principal and was getting my evaluation from my supervisor at the end of the year. I was fully prepared to get dinged on delegating too much authority. I cannot recall which year that was because I had exceptional associate principals who could work circles around me, so who knows?

Anyway, I thought I had delegated too much to my associate principal that year and that I was going to hear about it. To my amazement, I was told I had a low rating on delegation because I did not delegate ENOUGH! Wow. We debated the point a bit and came to consensus on his rating, and I was free to continue to delegate at a rate that I thought was borderline too much: win-win.

Another thing that comes to mind when I think of that boss: one day during a team meeting of all the leaders he proclaimed to me "it never looks like you are doing anything!" This caused guffaws around the room from my contemporaries. I also laughed and he immediately understood the magnitude of his claim. He followed it up with something like: "No, no, no. What I meant was you never look like you are doing anything, but everything is always done and done well." We all chuckled and I told my teammates "Remember, when your boss tells you it never looks like you are doing anything, that is a good thing!" Apparently, efficiency is one of my tenets, but it does not rise to the level of warranting a chapter in this book.

Owning it. The statement can be ambiguous and daunting. We are responsible for ourselves, our actions, and our words. I challenge all of you to consider your current situation. Do you own everything within your purview? You should because you will become a better version of yourself and you will bolster the trust others have in you.

TAKE CARE OF YOUR PEOPLE

I don't know if there is a rank order for my tenets, but as I think about this one, it sure seems like it might be the most important one. I previously explained my enneagram and that I am proud to say I am an 8: The Protector. It seems I come by this trait naturally, so I have a lot of examples of how it has manifested itself in my life.

To support the idea that taking care of my people is one of my prominent leadership tenets I am going to put into words the profound, extreme emotions I have had when visiting these locations: Ground Zero, Pearl Harbor, and the Pentagon. During the five times I have visited those sites (Ground Zero during the cleanup and after One World Trade Center was completed, Pearl Harbor twice, and the Pentagon after 9-11), I was overcome with emotion. I guess I could best describe my feelings as grief, indignation, sorrow, and failure. I think the first three emotions are self-explanatory and are most likely felt by most visitors to those sites.

The feeling of failure stands out to me because of how I view it. You see, I am not talking about the intelligence community's failure, just like I am not talking about our armed forces' failure. I am talking about my failure. I know this is irrational, because seriously, what could I have done to prevent any of those attacks? Most likely nothing. However, my drive to protect others is ingrained so deep in me that I feel as if I failed to protect those people who lost their lives. I know, this does not make much sense. Anyway, I guess I share this story so I may illustrate how important taking care of others is to me.

When I was in high school I went out for football as a 9th grader. Back then there were not any youth football leagues where I grew up, so playing organized tackle football was a new phenomenon and I didn't know much about it going into it. On day one of practice, the coach asked us who wanted to play offense and who wanted to play defense. I, like most of the guys, indicated a desire to play defense. Coach got mad and told us offense was where the glory was. That caused me to change my choice and I do not regret it because I found a position I was meant to play: left tackle.

If you have ever seen the movie Blind Side, you know the left tackle position. We had right-handed quarterbacks, thus, it was my job to protect their blindsides. I went on to play that position for four years and I prided myself in moving people off the ball and protecting everyone else on my team. It felt very natural to me.

As stated previously, I joined the US Army as a military police officer right out of high school. The Military Police Corps motto is "Assist, Protect, Defend." It seems like it was a natural fit for me. My propensity to protect others did not rise to my consciousness when I chose that job or subsequently did it for 9 years: I simply did my job which entailed defending the United States and protecting the American residents of military communities throughout the world. Looking back, I fondly remember the sense of self-worth I had because I was protecting others.

I had a personal interaction with General Colin Powell in early 1987 that reinforced the importance of taking care of your people. At that time General Powell was a Lieutenant General (LTG) and was the V Corps Commander in Frankfurt, West Germany. He commanded half of the United States Army forces that were in West Germany at the time with the other half being in the VII Corps headquartered in Stuttgart, West Germany.

One Friday night at about 2030 hours (that's 8:30 pm for you civilians) I was stationed outside of the command center of the Creighton W. Abrams Building in Frankfurt. LTG Powell's driver, Staff Sergeant (SSG) Otis Pearson, exited the command center doors and engaged me in a discussion. He outranked me considerably, and it was a one-sided conversation as he asked me a few questions about myself.

Moments later LTG Powell was making his way toward us and SSG Pearson opened the door for him. SSG Pearson then introduced me to him and told the general a little about me. A five-minute discussion ensued where we talked about my unit (the 109th Military Police Company), my home of record (Wisconsin), and what I wanted to do in life. I was in awe. Here it was, late on a Friday evening, and instead of going home, the commanding general was discussing my life with me, a lowly private!

Let me tell you, the importance of that lesson stuck

with me. Like many other leaders I had encountered by that time and have seen since General Powell could have ignored my existence by simply grunting acknowledgment to me when I told him to have a good evening. Instead, he took time out of what was the beginning of his weekend to make me feel as if I mattered. His simple questions showed me that he cared and that I was an important part of his command.

Taking care of my people became something upon which I consciously focused when I became an associate principal of a high school. I realized the health and welfare of the kids and adults in that building were my responsibility and I took it seriously. Perhaps the most tangible way that protecting others was present in my daily duties is when I encountered a behavioral issue within the school in which someone was a victim. When someone is victimized I feel compelled to help and protect them.

All too frequently, there is bullying in schools and when I encountered it I was less than happy. The last part of all the discussions that I had with bullies over the years entailed some admonitions of sorts: I warned the bullies that the behavior was done and I better not hear about them and/or their friends even talking about the victim(s). If I did, the repeat offenders typically understood me the second time.

I loved my time as an associate principal because the majority of my focus was on the kids. As they got to know me, they also got to know that I cared about them. I always interacted with them before, during, and after the school day and mutual respect was developed. With that respect came a lot of information. It was routine for me to hear about situations like drugs and alcohol in school soon after it arrived. Most kids wanted a clean school just like I did and my relationships with many of the kids encouraged them to work with me to keep it clean.

One of my favorite parts of my job as a school administrator was "spreading the love" on Fridays. I abhorred having appointments or anything else on my calendar on Fridays. Friday was my day to go and talk to my coworkers. It was commonplace to find me in classrooms and offices on Fridays simply shooting the breeze with my coworkers. Let me tell you, there are some awesome people in education in Wisconsin. You may hear on the news or have a personal experience with something like "School X is bad." I am here to tell you, that there are great educators in EVERY school in Wisconsin. None of them come to work on any given day thinking "how can I suck today?"

Anyway, as the years progressed spreading the love became something I did daily. Towards the end of my career in education, I made light of this practice with some coworkers and called what I was doing "wandering aimlessly." But seriously, this was when I was able to get to know my coworkers and show them I cared about who they are and what their life is like. I relished the hours I spent talking to my coworkers in their classrooms, the library, the lunchroom, etc. When I worked in education with my partners Dave and Mike, they took my idea of spreading the love on Fridays and did it together and called it a "victory lap." They both made lasting impressions on our coworkers and were able to be better leaders in the district, in part, because of this habit they started.

My daughter Kordan recently related a story to me about

a supervisor in her job. Kordan told me during a weekly check-in meeting, they focused on movies and television shows rather than on the job. Kordan thought this was great, and I told her I thought it was great leadership. That leader was getting to know Kordan on a personal level which will ultimately help her lead more effectively.

Checking on people and showing them love is something I do with the members of my professional network as well. The COVID-19 pandemic and subsequent shutdown of schools in Wisconsin in the spring of 2020 did not allow me to spread the love with other leaders that I normally would do at conferences and meetings. So, I incorporated a tactic that quite honestly, was somewhat selfish in nature: I made routine contact with people in my professional network throughout the country and checked in on them. I could tell by their reactions that my efforts were well-received, and I know these interactions helped us get through the isolation we were all experiencing.

Speaking of other administrators with whom I used to work: one of the ways I took care of them was to ensure they were involved in situations outside of their purview. This was selfish to some degree because I had more minds available to help me in sticky situations, but it was also a way I was able to take care of them. I bought into the idea that it was my job to help other leaders get ready for the next steps in their careers. Involving them in situations that weren't necessarily part of their job responsibilities was one of those ways. It is also how I wanted the schools to operate for the kids. Just like I wanted for the kids upon graduation, for the adults when it was time to make a career move, I wanted all of them to think "I want to do X,

AND I am prepared to do it!" Education and leadership are about opening up opportunities for people.

Taking care of my people in this manner allowed them to seek and earn the right to move up the career ladder in education. I was a high school principal for three years. Each of the first two years I had new associate principals who were stellar. Because I assisted them in their leadership growth, they were both promoted to other positions within the same district. My third associate principal, Mike, used his first year with me as a springboard to finding a district that was a better fit for him. Fast forward a couple of years and Mike parlayed his associate principal/athletic director experience into a director job with me. We then spent three years together and he worked closely with me daily as I was getting him ready for the next steps at the same time leaning on him to make me a better leader and our school a better place for the kids and our coworkers.

When I was a teacher I learned something that I still use today: I LISTEN and ACT when I ask people how they are doing. Initially, I did this without thinking about it. I became aware of my habit one day at the start of the second semester in my second year of teaching.

In the school in which I taught the kids' schedules could change at the end of the semester even though I taught a year-long course. So, at the start of the second semester, I had many kids that I had taught the first semester, mixed in with students I had not taught before. At the beginning of every class, I had a routine of asking "How is everyone doing today?" One day when I had asked that I heard a girl say "See, I told you he does that."

I asked her what she was talking about. Seriously, I

was ignorant of what she was referencing. She told me that when I ask the kids how they are doing I pay attention to the tones of voice and engage with the kids whose words may have been positive, but whose tones were not. I then spent a few moments engaged with those kids to ensure they were going to be ok.

I had no idea I did this until she pointed it out to her friend and then to me. I took that lesson to heart and to this day find myself calling BS when someone uses words professing positivity while using a tone of voice that tells me otherwise. If you stop and observe you will constantly hear people ask "how are you doing?" but then rarely, if ever, sincerely listen to the response. Start listening.

Recently I was featured in a newsletter from a state organization and one of the questions they asked me for the profile was "What advice do you have for those working in HR?" My answer in part was "When negative situations occur, treat people well." When you treat people well, even the most egregious of situations can end amicably.

I have taught this to others over the years by utilizing the phrase "bring them full circle." When a negative situation occurs, it is very easy to get caught up in the situation and let negative emotions dedicate how the situation plays out. By bringing people full circle, I allow people to have the full range of emotions that may come and eventually we get back to the situation at hand. When people can work through all of those emotions, rational thought usually returns and they can see the situation for what it is which allows for a more acceptable outcome.

Taking care of your people has the side benefit of earning you respect. I discovered early on in my school administrator career how showing kids respect, including when they are involved in disciplinary situations, not only showed them I cared but also earned me respect. Here is a typical manner in which I discussed discipline with a kid:

Me: "So, what do you think your consequence should be?"

Kid: "I don't know."

Me.: "Well, it can't be nothing, and it sure doesn't rise to expulsion level, so what do you think?"

At this point, I had not decided on what I should do and I would always let the kid dictate where we started the negotiation. If the response back to me was something like "A couple of detentions, I guess." I always took at least one away from their first proposal by saying something like "A couple sounds a little steep to me. How does one sound?" Kids always agreed to my lowball offers. They then grabbed candy off my desk, thanked me, and left my office.

I realized I was on to something when I had kid after kid leave my office thanking me for discipline consequences so I assumed this approach could be taken with adults.

Earlier, I described how I spread the love. Because I focused on that, it made situations in which I was discussing discipline with adults a little better and easier. There were two particular individuals in one of my former districts whose behavior rose to the level of having to be disciplined. Upon leaving my office with a letter of reprimand in hand, each of them thanked me. To this day when I see them, I get big hugs from them.

Surprisingly, not all leaders understand the tenet "take care of your people". When I was a new associate principal I worked with a veteran principal who was working in his second district. On the morning of the first day of school, I informed him we were going to take a tour of the school at the end of the day and check in on the five or six new teachers who started that day. I recall he gave me a quizzical look as he accepted my proposal.

At the end of the school day, I found him and reminded him of our task and we set out to accomplish it. As we were walking to the nearest room that had a new teacher, my principal asked me "Why are we doing this again?" I was dumbfounded. Most of our new people that year were right out of college and had just taught for real for the first time. I guarantee you at least a couple of them were rethinking their career choices based on the experiences of that first day.

I had to inform him that it was our job to take care of our teachers, especially the new ones, on day #1. We completed our task and called it a day. Just recalling that discussion makes me shake my head.

As my career in education progressed I ensured all of the other leaders with whom I worked knew the importance of checking on our new hires on day #1. Some got it without me telling them it was important, but I could tell by some reactions that the importance I placed on this responsibility was met with skepticism. Funnily (yes, that is a word that I learned from a very intelligent coworker, thank you Mrs. Judson) enough, towards the end of my career I often crossed paths with various other leaders at the culmination of the first day of school because we were all making our rounds checking on the new people. Refreshing.

Greeting Cards. No, this is not a paid endorsement for Hallmark, but rather a discussion about the importance of sending people cards as a way to take care of them. Early on in my career as a school administrator, I learned that it was powerful and logical to send cards to coworkers when significant events occurred like the birth of a child, the death of a loved one, a serious health issue, etc. So, I did it. I thought of myself as a Sunshine Committee of one. I continued this approach my entire career in school administration. I was fortunate enough over the years to have coworkers who were connected to the flow of information within all the districts I worked and they would tell me of the need for a card.

Eventually, I broadened my use of cards to include sending "thank yous" to people and I subsequently brought this practice to the leadership team at one of our monthly meetings. By that time, we had already started the practice of starting each meeting by sharing success stories and celebrations. It was a very natural fit for us to incorporate thank you cards into our routine. So, for the remainder of my career in education, we spent about 10 minutes at the beginning of every leadership team meeting sharing celebrations while each of us wrote one or several thank you cards to coworkers.

I know the practice of sending cards made an impact. Recipients knew we were being sincere when we sent them and it was very routine to receive emails thanking us for the "thank you" we had given. Our coworkers knew by our actions that we cared.

I had one particular acknowledgment of a card about five years ago that stuck with me. I was attending a social engagement with people from a district in which I had at one time worked. The spouse of one of my former coworkers was there and he expressed regret that his wife (my former coworker) could not attend the event because she really would have wanted to see me. He went on to explain the depth of gratitude she had for me because of the simple act of sending a card to her and her family when she had given birth years before. You see, this particular coworker was a bit introverted and therefore did not have a whole lot of positive, personal relationships with other adults in the district. When she gave birth I was one of the few who acknowledged it and she sensed my sincerity and never forgot.

Early on in my tenure as a district administrator, action by the state government caused the teachers' union to dissolve. This caused one of my coworkers to storm into my office where a hilarious interaction (at least to me) ensued. Apparently, this coworker had been part of the Sunshine Committee that was developed by the members of the local teacher union. She explained their various tasks with the most important aspect of their role being sending condolence and congratulatory cards to coworkers when something occurred. Due to the dissolution of the union she very forcefully and a bit disrespectfully told me that it was now my job to take over the work of that union-based committee. She had thrown down the gauntlet and was ready for a fight. I sort of chuckled which caused her to get her dander up a bit and I told her "I am already doing that." She did not know what to say. She came in spoiling for a fight and left without finding an outlet for her aggression. Taking care of my people saved the day.

I think I am making it clear that taking care of your people should be one of your top priorities. This seems to be the first lens I use most of the time. Over the years as a district administrator people asked me "What is the worst part of your job?" Most were surprised when I replied with "Snow Days!" Outside of the obvious issue of being wrong all the time in some people's eyes, snow, ice, and extreme cold issues caused me all sorts of stress. Due to my propensity to take care of others, these days hit home with me.

Snowy and icy roads, extreme temperatures of -25° and colder, and wind chills of -35° and colder always present a safety concern, and deciding on whether or not to close school caused me grief. Closing was usually innocuous and I would still receive the hate emails and tweets, but I could live with those. It was when I didn't close school, that the internal strife occurred. You see, I always worry about kids and adults traveling to/from school, and if I did not cancel school and there was a bad accident due to hazardous road conditions, I do not know what I would have done.

This desire to protect everyone else is so strong that I even got stressed when I heard sirens around the start or end of any school day. My immediate thoughts were "What is the issue and is everyone safe?" There were only a few minor issues over the years, so I consider myself lucky.

Comparable to my emotional response to snow days was my response to COVID-19. When the COVID-19 pandemic shut down most of the country, including the school district in which I was working in March 2020, I felt HELPLESS. It is my number one priority to keep those in my charge, in this case, all of the kids and the employees in the district, safe. I knew that I could not do that and it was very emotional. Like everyone else, I had never been in a pandemic before, but I knew there were going to be people who were hurt both physically and mentally because of it. I thought about all of my coworkers and the kids who were used to constant social interaction in school, with some kids going home to their rooms and not coming in physical contact with anyone. I knew we had kids who were not safe at home and lacked some of the basic necessities like food, heat, and love. And here we were telling them to go to the one place from which they hoped to escape daily. It appears we are coming out of the pandemic and hundreds of thousands of Americans are dead and countless studies attribute a growing mental health crisis to the pandemic. My fears came to fruition and I still feel helpless.

This same feeling of helplessness and emotional response occurred during the social justice movement that I referenced in an earlier chapter. It is hard for me to put into words the depth of emotion I feel when I see others treated poorly or discriminated against due to things out of their control, like skin color, ethnicity, gender identity, and sexual orientation. I know I can only support the effort to negate the inequities, but I struggle with the fact that some people chose to discriminate against others due to something out of that person's control. Baffling.

In addition to how you treat people, the setting of said treatment occurs can be viewed through the lens of protecting your people. One of the many important things I learned from my wife, Kori, is that everyone should be treated with the same level of respect. I am conscious of this all the time and it is even on my mind when I enter a client's place of business. The receptionist is just as import-ant as the chief executive officer with whom I am going to meet and I show that with the respect I give each of them.

I couple this idea with another approach that I take with people: meet them on their turf. In one of my classes for my master's degree, I had a wise, former principal and current school board member as a professor. This guy reminded me of an old midwestern farmer: he was intelligent, animated, and engaging, and spoke in informal English. During one lecture he was giving us advice about how to handle personnel-related situations with people.

As I said, he was very animated, so he set up a table in the front of the room and had a volunteer sit at the table while he sat with his back to the class. He then demonstrated how he would interact with the person. He used statements that make me chuckle to this day: "Sometimes you have to hug them and sometimes you have to spank them." After he said this he acted out the hugging by sitting on the same side of the table as the volunteer to show us he was providing emotional support. He then demonstrated the "spanking" by very animatedly running to the other side of the table and sitting down, thus creating a barrier with the table.

Well, I took this lesson to heart and utilize it to this day. When I am involved in a personnel issue I always consider the setting of the interaction because I view the manipulation of the setting as a way to take care of my people. Most of the time personnel issues can be resolved with a discussion. Because of this, the vast majority of the ones that I have held over the years have occurred on someone else's turf.

I am sure some of you can relate to being "called on the carpet," and the negative emotions that occur when this happens. From my experience, calling someone on the carpet can hamper a positive resolution at times: the person with whom I am interacting is so upset about being in my office that a beneficial discussion cannot take place. So, instead, I tend to go to others' workspaces to have these types of discussions. When I go on someone else's turf, they are in control and are not at a disadvantage. This approach has worked wonders over the years and has allowed me to resolve many personnel issues with a simple chat.

Despite my preferred approach, some situations have warranted me "calling people on the carpet" due to the egregious nature of the situation or because I simply wanted to ensure my point was made. You see, most disciplinary issues do not have to result in some type of paperwork. At times, a verbal admonishment or reprimand is enough. When I encounter situations in which it warrants more than a chat on their turf but does not rise to the level of formal discipline, the only thing I discipline the person with is dealing with the stress of coming to my turf. Severe, egregious situations, by default, were always on my turf.

Regardless of the situation or the locale of the discussion, I always talk to others in a straightforward, casual manner. One of the other leaders in my professional network used the phrase "living room talk" when he was describing this type of interaction. The goal of interaction in a personnel-related situation is to resolve it. By keeping it real and talking to someone with real talk, as if you are chatting in your living room, you can de-escalate most situations.

One time I used real-talk with someone and I shocked him. At that particular time, there was a rather public, heated personnel situation occurring. One of my coworkers obviously and vociferously supported the person at the heart of this situation. Due to this ardent support, I was, by default, the enemy. This situation lasted for about a month before it was resolved and in the middle of it, I happened to come face to face with this staunch supporter of my coworker. I asked him to step to the side of the group with me so that we could talk a bit privately. I could tell by the look on his face the last thing he wanted to be doing was talking to me.

I asked him one simple question: "What can I do to help you stop hating me?" He stammered on his words and was shocked that I called him out on his feelings toward me. He went on to explain his support of his coworker and how he was a good employee. I agreed with him, thanked him for his support of his coworker, and told him that I support our coworker as well. However, I also told him some things needed to be addressed and that it was my job to do so. He seemed to understand and our relationship improved dramatically after that. We worked together for another six or seven years and he reciprocated the respect I showed him.

As I mentioned earlier when I discussed checking on others during the pandemic, taking care of other people can also allow you to reap some benefits. From 1992 to 1993 I was the police desk sergeant for the military police station on Fort Clayton, in the Republic of Panamá. It was 3 years after the United States' invasion of Panama in which we arrested their president, Manuel Noriega for drug trafficking offenses, and as you could probably assume, tensions in the city were high at times.

As the desk sergeant, it was my job to oversee and

coordinate the efforts of the various military police officers that were on patrol, and that included the following: gate guards, vehicle patrols, bike patrols, jungle (foot) patrols, military police investigations, liaisons who worked in Panama City with Panamanian National Police partners, and investigators from the Army's Criminal Investigation Command (CID). At any given time there are upwards of 80 patrols/individuals on duty. This was not a one-person job and I had two assistants: an RTO (radio/telephone operator) who was the dispatcher, and a desk clerk who formalized all of the reports for 24 hours into a document called a blotter. For part of my tenure as the desk sergeant, I had the honor of working with a desk clerk named Specialist Mark E. Gutting from Grand Rapids, MI.

Specialist Gutting and I sat about six feet apart for 12 hours a day four to six days a week for about a year. We talked all of the time and when things were slow, he often started talking about bass fishing back home with his folks. Despite being a few years younger than him, I was his supervisor. We were not friends, but rather positive, professional teammates.

Specialist Gutting eventually came down on orders and was sent back stateside in 1993 where he ended up in a unit that was being deployed to Somalia which was mired in a Civil War. During his time on the police desk with me, Specialist Gutting became tight with our RTO, Specialist Phillips. He and Phillips were close enough that when he was deployed to Somalia, Gutting listed Phillips on his contact list in case he was killed in action.

Specialist Phillips and I were working when the call came in notifying Specialist Phillips that Specialist Gutting had just been killed in action. I absorbed the news, showed my support for Specialist Phillips, and moved on. Or so I thought.

About six years ago (2016), I followed through on a long-overdue task that I had committed to back in 1993: I tracked down Specialist Gutting's mom and called her. We spoke for quite a while and she was shocked to hear about the job her son had when he worked with me. Apparently, she was surprised to learn that he had the skills to create the blotter that was viewed daily by every one of authority in the United States Army in Panamá. I could hear the pride in her voice. I regret not calling her sooner to enlighten her about how valuable a teammate I had in her son.

Little did I know that call was going to help me as well. You see, for years I cringed internally and felt uncomfortable when someone thanked me or acknowledged my service in any manner. I was never offended, put off, or upset about the gratitude, but rather I was simply uncomfortable. About a year after that phone call I realized I had changed: I no longer felt ill at ease when someone brought up my veteran status and I even found myself welcoming questions and engaging in discussions about my service. I eventually put two and two together: that phone call had helped me heal when I didn't even know I needed it. It provided me closure and permitted me to be proud of my service. Since then, I have even gone so far as to get the military police crossed pistols (their logo) tattooed on my side.

How you take care of your people depends on a lot: your situation, your leadership skills, your values, the people you are leading, the size of your organization, etc. Regardless of who you are and what your situation is, you can take active steps to take care of your people. This will help you make a connection with them and improve your reputation as a leader. And as I have shown you, taking care of others can help you while you are helping them. Sometime in the next seven days, Friday will come around and I challenge all of you to spread some love!

ACTIONS SPEAK LOUDER THAN WORDS

Allowing my actions to speak louder than my words is something of which I have always been conscious as an adult. I know my actions will make an impact long before my words will. Back in 2010 when I started down this path of self-discovery I was immediately able to identify this is how I operate, but I could not figure out why I adhered to this leadership tenet. For years I reflected on this and still could not figure out where I learned it.

In 2016 I was speaking to someone with whom I had grown up and we were discussing leadership and our youth. The other person happened to mention one of our coaches by name. Eureka! I figured out why I bought into letting my actions speak louder than my words. You see, our high school football team was relatively good when we were in school and we won a lot of games. Because of this, our coach stressed to us the importance of not getting caught up in the trash-talking or retaliating to cheap shots that came our way. He simply said, "let the scoreboard speak for you."

Now, he did not mean for us to say to our opponents "Hey, look at the scoreboard, Losers!" He simply expected us to hustle back to the huddle and not say a word despite the taunting and cheap shots we incurred. This lesson stuck with me and I still let the proverbial scoreboard do my talking.

Some leaders utilize an open door policy as a way to show others they are available to them. Well, let me tell you, I hate this idea because it feels like an easy solution that does not get to the heart of the problem. If you have to tell people you have an open door policy, you most likely do not have a good rapport with your coworkers.

I can't count the times I have said to my coworkers "If you have questions, ask!" I was frequently taken up on this offer. As I mentioned earlier, I like to "spread the love," which started on Fridays at the beginning of my career and turned into a manner in which I led 24/7. My coworkers knew I was there for them and did not need a policy that said my door was open so they could come and talk to me. Organic, spontaneous conversations are better than any appointment I could find on my calendar.

I worked with another administrator once and we had a chat about an open door policy that he had used in the past. Well, his policy bit him in the keister when he closed his door once so he could accomplish a task without getting interrupted. Word quickly spread that he did not want to hear from anyone because, despite his policy, his door was closed! Oh, the scandal! Newsflash: it's not about the door, people! Show your people you are there for them; you don't need the policy to tell them that.

Now that I write about open door policies, I realize the

fact they are not needed because being there for you people takes care of the need. Thus, two of my tenets, Take Care of Your People, and Actions Speak Louder than Words, are related, and unfortunately, can have unintended results

I was one to two years into my role as high school principal when one of the elementary principals with whom I worked came to talk to me and she had her dander up. At the commencement of our meeting she laid into me about several issues that were occurring in her school and the fact that as she was dealing with them, my name repeatedly came up. I was a bit confused for two reasons: 1) why did my name come up? And 2) Why did that cause a problem? So, I asked her. She then unleashed a tirade about how I had helped some of her people and she ended by asking me "Why do my people keep coming to you?"

Ah, I understood the issue. As an associate principal and principal for the previous two or three years, I had led by taking care of my people and letting my actions speak for themselves. It was routine for me to help my coworkers in my school with personal and/or professional issues. Well, word got out and I found myself interacting with educators from other schools within the district. It was normal for me to field phone calls and receive visitors from other schools at the end of the school day. I didn't overstep my bounds, but simply coached people through their problems/issues and let them discover their own solutions. I was good at it. Unfortunately, this principal did not like that because she kept hearing things like "When I talked to Mr. Kopp..." and "Well, Mr. Kopp helped me realize..." She was furious! Apparently, at the same time, her people started coming to me for coaching and mentoring, and they stopped going to her. She viewed me as usurping her power. I simply viewed it as taking care of people.

Sometimes one's adherence to their tenets can waiver, and reminders come along that reinforce them. I had one such moment several years ago. We had a sports issue that caused a whole lot of people in the community to be upset. If you have ever worked in education you know the magnitude of feelings that come out when high school sports are the topic. Anyway, this situation was near to being resolved and two other administrators and I held a meeting with community members, kids, parents, and coaches about the issue. It was intense and negative emotions were running high.

What I witnessed that day shocked me. There were members of our community, both parents and kids who I had previously respected, screaming at us as we hosted the meeting. To make matters worse, the other two leaders who were with me reciprocated and screamed back! Wow. It was a surreal moment for me. I was between the two of them and they took turns screaming back at people who had just screamed at us. I was a participant in the conversation, and when it was my turn, I simply spoke loud enough so that all who were present could hear me. I did not scream or show anger.

The situation was resolved a couple of weeks after that, but the ramifications stuck around. For several months I had random conversations with coworkers and community members about the situation and every single one of them referred to the meeting we had hosted and how terrible the behavior was of the other two leaders with whom I worked.

Ironically, my propensity for holding people accountable had caused the situation in the first place, but due to my deportment throughout the situation, I came off as a winner, whereas my contemporaries had their images tarnished. I don't know if I needed that lesson about the importance of letting my actions speak for themselves, but I am sure the reminder did not hurt.

When I became a district administrator (superintendent) I was fortunate to be hired in a geographical area in which there was a cluster of districts with a lot of good people who were my contemporaries. I met monthly with the 10 other leaders from neighboring districts for 2-3 hours and we discussed logistics, politics as they related to public education, and educational issues. I was very conscious of the fact that I was still wet behind the ears, so initially, I listened a lot and spoke very little. Towards the end of my first year, we were discussing a specific educational issue and some were perplexed about how to proceed. I shared how I had led on that issue in my district and my approach was met with appreciation.

After that meeting, the venerable veteran of the group, who happened to lead and host the monthly meetings, asked me to stay after as others were taking their leave. Now, this particular person had been in education for nearly 40 years and had been in his role as district administrator for over 25 years. We had not spoken a lot personally before that meeting, and I stayed after, a little perplexed about the topic of our upcoming tete-a-tete.

He started the interaction by stating something like "I wasn't sure about you. You never talk much. But now! Now I see why you were hired. You know what you're doing!" Fast forward another year and it and this same leader decided it was time for him to give up the proverbial gavel of the group and he turned to me to take over. That was one of the most surprising moments of my professional career. Here I was, a relatively new district administrator and I had just been picked to lead the group by the leader who had been doing it for more than two decades. I was lower in tenure than most of the rest of the group, but my deportment and actions allowed me to become the leader of that group.

I frequently discuss general leadership and my tenets with those I lead and when we focus on actions speaking louder than words, specifically, I tell them it is more important to be a winner than it is to win. In any situation, there are usually winners and losers. Yes, winning is nice, but I would argue being a winner is better. We have all seen, or maybe even have been guilty of, someone being a sore winner. Sore winning rankles me more than someone who is a sore loser. When you win, your actions can speak for themselves: there is no need to gloat, taunt, brag, etc., but we have all seen it. When you lose, you can lose with grace, which can be very powerful.

Several years ago I discussed this very topic with a softball coach with whom I worked. Several years before that discussion his team had lost in the state championship game. His players could have retreated to the dugout by storming off the field in defeat and ignoring the winners. This did not happen. Instead, as the state championship team members were receiving their awards, his players stood on the diamond and applauded them, albeit with tears streaming down their faces. I told him I appreciated that and thanked him. He was taken aback and told me "I didn't tell them to do that!" Our discussion continued and he realized that he had set them up to be winners even when they lost.

He then realized the importance of the lessons he taught when he recounted the experience he and his players had after winning the semi-final game in that same tournament: the opposing players went through the post-game congratulatory line and were punching his and his players' hands, rather than shaking them. They made their ire over their defeat very obvious to all: it was palpable. He realized their coach probably did not tell them to punch the hands of their opponents but rather had acted in such a manner throughout the season, that they thought the behavior was appropriate. That team in the semifinal game lost the game and came off as losers. Whereas, our kids lost the championship game but came off the diamond as winners.

When one focuses on being a winner, winning is a natural byproduct.

At times the messages you want your actions to send are political. No, not the democrat/republican politics, but rather the politics of relationships. Two stories come to mind on this one. Back when I was a principal I had to deal with some behavioral issues, especially the high-profile issues that involved drugs in school. I had this one situation in which we had caught a student with cocaine because two of this student's friends came to me separately within minutes of one another to tell me she was "All G'd up!" and the "Cocaine is in her truck in the parking lot." They both pleaded with me to find the cocaine and bust the student, thus giving her the wake-up call she needed to get clean.

Well, we found the cocaine and addressed it with the

student. That night around midnight I was still working, yes, unfortunately, there are 24 hours in a day in which work can be done. Anyway, while I was going through some work emails I received a new one from the mother of the student in question in which she lambasted me for my interference in her kid's life. The email was a power move by the mom in an attempt to intimidate and/or get me to back off. Now, I could have sat on that email until the next morning, but I chose to do a power move myself by replying shortly after midnight, mere minutes after her email had been sent. The intent of my actions, to wit, the immediate response via email, was meant to send her a message that I was not intimidated by her, the situation, or her attorney. The board of education subsequently held the student accountable for the use and possession of cocaine on school grounds.

Another example of my actions sending a message involved negotiations with the teachers' union. Please do not think that I am anti-union. I know they have their place and have done some positive things for members, and I benefited from a union when I was in it. Anyway, I was asked to get involved in negotiations of a collectively bargained agreement (the union contract) because the board and the union had been at an impasse for 2+ years and the members of the board thought I could bring the sides together. The meeting started at 6 pm and present were 3 board members, two district-level administrators, 4 teachers who were bargaining on behalf of the rest of the teacher union members, and me. I liked and professionally respected everyone who was in that room, so despite being arduous, the meeting was rather amicable. The meeting lasted for a long time, but we were able to come to an agreement and we parted ways at 2:30 am.

At 7:30 am, a mere five hours later, I decided to show the teachers from the previous night's meeting that I respected them and viewed them as valuable teammates by greeting them at the door when they came in. By that time of my tenure, I knew roughly what time each of them arrived and through which doors. So, I positioned myself near each of those doors at the appropriate time and welcomed them back to the school. My salutations and efforts were met with appreciation and it solidified my status as a leader. As the years progressed, my relationship with those teachers was very positive and valuable to me.

Words are simply that: words. They are easy to use and can make things seem as they aren't. Words can be shallow and ambiguous. Actions are what matter. The conscious effort put into one's actions as a leader can pay dividends for years. People may forget your words, but they will never forget your actions. Don't talk, act.

ACCOUNTABILITY

Accountability is a tough one: literally and figuratively. Accountable to my teammates, to the organization, and my customers. It is never-ending. I do not think I consciously lead with accountability in mind all the time. When I reflect, I do acknowledge that accountability is important to me, so I struggle with why I am not always aware of it when I do it.

Accountability sure seems to me like it is about rules, first and foremost. I think one of the first times I thought about rules and accountability was when I was stationed in Fort Devens, MA, as a military police officer from 1990-1991. I was assigned to the Fort Devens Military Police Company; sorry, it didn't have a fancier name than that. Right around that same time, Massachusetts enacted a new law about domestic disturbances: if law enforcement officers responded to a domestic disturbance, they were required to remove someone from the scene.

A typical domestic disturbance occurs in a place of residence and is usually between a man and a woman who are in some type of domestic relationship. So, odds were such that when we were dispatched to a domestic we were headed into someone's home and by law, once I got there, someone had to leave. This is not to say that I had to arrest someone, which did occur on occasion, but rather, I just had to make one of the people involved in the situation leave the abode so I could ensure the domestic situation was over and everyone would be safe; at least temporarily, anyway. I had to respond to countless domestics during my time at Fort Devens and I have never been able to shake the uncomfortable feeling I get when I think about them.

Yet another time that accountability played a role in my military career was early in 1990 while I was still in Germany in the 109th Military Police Company. Accountability in this example was not the driving factor, but rather safety was. That year my company was part of REFORGER (RETurn of FORces to GERmany) 1990: Centurion Shield. REFORGER, as the name implies, was a military exercise in which NATO (North Atlantic Treaty Organization) member nations deployed military units to West Germany to practice and ensure they had the capability of deploying in case World War III broke out with any member of the Eastern Bloc of nations. Most units were from the United States with some other random units thrown in, typically from the United Kingdom and Canada.

During Centurion Shield my company was tasked with guarding the field residences of VIPs who were involved in the exercise as leaders and/or observers. By that time I was a non-commissioned officer and was assigned as the dayshift supervisor for one of the gasthauses, a tavern/ inn that dotted the landscape in Germany and was being used as a temporary residence for the exercise. We arrived there on a Saturday or Sunday and started guarding the place. Our dayshift contingent worked a 12-hour shift from 0600-1800 hours daily. The duty was rather monotonous and boring. Having said that, when you are guarding something/someone, boring is safe, so I am OK with boring.

Anyway, our first VIP was scheduled to arrive around 1500hrs (3 pm) on Friday of that week. Around 1100 hours that Friday morning, one of my patrols, Specialist D. Luke Hall, called me on the handheld radio to inform me that a roach coach (food truck) had just set up shop right in front of the gasthaus. I went out to the front corner of the building and met up with Specialist Hall where we observed the person working in the truck. Within minutes of arriving, he started selling food to passersby. I let this occur for a few more minutes, but my gut was telling me something was up. I couldn't help but think about how the town square had been calm and quiet all week with nary a food truck around, and a mere few hours before the arrival of our first VIP, one shows up and parks RIGHT IN FRONT of the gasthaus we were guarding?!

Specialist Hall and I repositioned ourselves inside the gasthaus near windows overlooking the town square and this food truck. I called the situation in. It took about 45 minutes, but it seemed like 1-2 hours elapsed before something happened. During this time, Specialist Hall and I continued our surveillance of the food truck and its sole occupant. Business was by no means bustling, but there had been a steady flow of customers while we were conducting surveillance.

And then it happened: seemingly out of nowhere 12-15 members of the West German Kriminal Polizei (KRIPO), all armed to the teeth with pistols and submachine guns, appeared out of nowhere and took down the occupant of the truck. Within another 30 minutes, all evidence of the situation was erased from the town, including the truck. Later that evening we got word that the driver/owner of the truck happened to have a permit to sell fish sandwiches at that location for a few hours around midday every Friday. We were wrong in what we thought was going on, but right to focus on accountability and call it in. Specialist Hall was awarded an Army Achievement Medal for his actions that day.

One of the things I learned as a school administrator was if I didn't hold people accountable, others interpreted my lack of action as condoning the actions of the offender. So, I held people accountable. What I experienced from this was interesting. Take a moment to reflect on the chapter regarding taking care of your people. I mentioned this was prevalent in my mind when I was holding someone accountable. I also strove to treat people with respect and never lost my cool. This approach allowed people to focus on the situation at hand and not focus on me, the messenger. Most of the time these situations ended amicably and we were able to move on from the situation.

Others' reactions were the things of note. A small minority of stakeholders viewed my actions as heavy-handed and unnecessary. I got a reputation as a grim reaper. The vast majority of others viewed my actions as a sign of commitment to the school and district. They saw that I was not going to tolerate people who broke rules and/ or underperformed, which ultimately hurt the kids. Those who viewed my actions as positive were reinvigorated and recommitted to the institution.

Some of my fellow administrators have seen me in action over the years when I have dealt with contentious personnel and student issues to ensure accountability. In these meetings, I focus on a lot of things, but it always comes back to treating those on the other side of the table with respect. One of my fellow principals back in the day was in awe at my approach and the subsequent, typical, positive reactions by those I held accountable. Eventually, he started referring to me as the Velvet Hammer. Moral of the story: you can hold people accountable and show them respect at the same time.

Several years ago I was meeting with my team and one of my teammates explained to the rest of the team how he and I had a discussion and he now knew he was wrong about something and had to fix it.

One of the other leaders said something like "Let me guess. Dan stood beside you for a while and told you that you were wrong without actually telling you that you were wrong. Correct?" The other person chuckled and said that is exactly what happened. I had to engage with both of them and asked them to clarify their points of view because I was befuddled. Based on the ensuing conversation with all members of the team, it seems that I tend to coach all the time and help people acknowledge and fix their issues. I will take that as a compliment!

Accountability isn't always about negative behavior. At times it can manifest itself in other forms. I think back to a job interview I had with a school board of education and I stressed the importance of accountability. I explained to them that it was not just accountability of those who may work for me, but the reverse was true as well: I was accountable to the people who worked for me as well, just like I was accountable to the board and the kids in the district. Similarly, I stressed the importance of their role and how they were accountable to the taxpayers, kids, employees, and the community.

Accountability to others is important in all aspects of life and perhaps has become more prevalent in my mind as I look at society in the last five years. Somewhere along the line, being civil to one another in this country has become less important. Several years ago it became trendy to not be "politically correct." When I saw this happening, I immediately thought "political correctness" is not the right way to look at what is going on. Instead, we should be looking at accountability to one another through the lens of civility.

One very odd thing comes to mind: the statement "Merry Christmas." I am not a Christian and do not practice religion. Having said that, I have always appreciated and understood someone's intent when they give me the greeting "Merry Christmas." I was never offended, put off, or irritated. I knew the person saying or writing it was simply sending me positive holiday vibes; negative intent was never assumed.

Now, however, it has become trendy to, for lack of a better way to look at it, rub people's faces in the statement Merry Christmas. It is commonplace to see headlines on the news or overhear the statement in public and it is laden in sarcasm and contempt. This is downright baffling to me. When and why did wishing someone warm feelings and thoughts during the holiday season become weaponized? We lost our civility and have lost our accountability to each other.

Masks due to the pandemic. Don't get me started on these. Now that we are coming out of a global pandemic that has killed millions around the world, how and why did we lose our collective mind in this country and turn the wearing of masks into a political issue? Masks are recommended for use and were mandated in some places to keep those around you safe from you in case you were contagious. That is what accountability to others is all about. I yield to pedestrians in crosswalks, I drive on the correct side of the road, and I don't blare my music at 3 am and wake up my household and neighbors. Why? Because I care about others and am accountable to them. It is my civic responsibility to respect others and not put them in harm's way, or in the case of loud music, bother them in the middle of the night. The fact that we cannot agree that the wearing of masks is important to protect those around us is ludicrous to me

Accountability is more than just ensuring those who work for you are adhering to the rules of your organization. It also involves how we need to be cognizant of those around us and ensure that we treat them civilly. Could you imagine if accountability was a leadership tenet everyone embraced? I would love to experience that.

BE BEYOND REPROACH

The concept of being beyond reproach always gives me pause and causes a chuckle. Back when I was teaching, I worked with a guy who asked me to write him a letter of recommendation. I think the world of this guy: he is a wholesome, all-American father and husband, and is one of the best educators with whom I have been blessed to work. I was honored to be asked to write the letter and easily accomplished the task. Upon reading the letter, my coworker quoted part of it to me: "His deportment is beyond reproach!" He then said "Wow! This is a good letter. Just so we're clear, 'deportment being beyond reproach' is a good thing, right?" I trust you now understand why this one makes me chuckle.

Being beyond reproach simply means that you act in such a manner that you give others no reason to question your morals, ethics, or motives.

Regardless of your position in life, whether you are in a leadership position or not, conducting yourself so that you are beyond reproach should be something for which you strive daily. Here is how I explain it to other leaders with whom I work: if we were to act inappropriately in one area, whether our behavior was immoral, unethical, or illegal, and then get scrutinized and questioned about our behavior, decisions, etc., in another area, we deserve that scrutiny and we have a problem on our hands that is of our own making.

However, if we always act in a moral, ethical, and legal manner and get scrutinized and questioned about things, that is not our problem, but rather it is the problem of the people who are looking for something that is not there. If we do things inappropriately, we are guilty as charged. If we don't, we can walk with our heads held high knowing we did the right thing.

When I was in high school I took to heart the lessons imparted my way by my various coaches. As is the case now, it was routine for kids to dress up on game day. It set me in a mind-frame that got me ready to compete that night. Additionally, this practice put my teammates and me in the spotlight. I knew that our attire made us stand out and made it obvious we were part of the team. I knew people were watching us and we were representing the school. I took that seriously and did not want to bring dishonor to the school, the team, or myself with stupid behavior.

I guess this same idea is true when I contemplate the code of conduct that high school athletes then, and now, adhere to. Alcohol and other drugs are forbidden, along with the mandate that appropriate behavior is a must in all facets of a young athlete's life. Not only did I want to preserve my reputation by not acting foolish and doing things that were against the code, but I also considered the impact my actions could have had on my team. This concept, quite obviously, links back to the accountability tenet. I did not want to do anything that put my eligibility in question because I did not want to let my coaches and teammates down. All of us had a role to play on the team and all of us mattered. Thus, had I been kicked off the team, others would suffer due to my absence. That would not have been fair to them and I knew that. Now, let me tell you some stories of my escapades in high school once football was done my senior year. Well actually, that is for another book.

When I entered the military, "military bearing" was stressed by the various drill sergeants during basic and advanced individual training. This was nothing more than acting appropriately and professionally while in uniform (I guess, when not in uniform too, for that matter!). I immediately understood and embraced the concept because I knew that I not only represented myself, but also my company, the United States Army, and the United States of America. The stakes are high when you are serving. One of the lessons I learned that was reinforced in the various units in which I served was that of being "squared away" when it came to my appearance. This meant that my hair was cut appropriately, I was clean-shaven, my uniform was pressed, and my boots were shined. To this day I am still the best ironer in my home and frequently iron my wife's clothes.

I think most adults can relate to the concept of being squared away due to our own experiences. I am sure all of you have seen someone in authority, whether it is in uniform or simply in your place of business, who looked disheveled. Whether you are conscious of your reaction or not, your mind has dismissed a disheveled person to some degree because of how he or she has presented themselves.

When we encounter someone in authority, we assume certain characteristics are going to be prevalent: appropriate attire, well-groomed, and apparent intelligence when communicating. When people don't exude these characteristics, their authority is somewhat diminished.

Here is how I explain this concept to others when I am teaching a leadership class or working with leaders: picture yourself observing a group of law enforcement officers who are providing security at an event you are attending. As you observe them you see them clustered in groups, swilling coffee, while some are lounging against walls or sitting down. You may think nothing of that, which is my exact point: the people who those officers are there protecting you from won't think anything of them either.

Contrast that picture in your mind to another scene: you are at the same event and you see law enforcement officers along the perimeter of the area, spread out, with their eyes roving the crowd. Periodically, you see a roving patrol make contact with each of the sentries to check-in and assess the security in any given zone. In which scenario do you take the security of that event more seriously? You, along with anyone who may wish to do someone harm, are going to determine the law enforcement officials in the second scenario are much more capable of keeping you safe due to their deportment.

Here is an example of how I encountered deportment that caused me to judge people negatively. Full disclosure, I can judge, and judge hard: it is one of my shortcomings and this is an example of when I did it. Anyway, about four years ago, my wife, daughter, and I were traveling on a two-lane US Highway around 8 am. It was winter, the temperature was hovering around 0 degrees, there was snow and ice on the road, and we were in the middle of the morning commute: the road was filled with school buses, semi-trailers, and personal vehicles.

As we were driving in a long string of traffic at about 55 miles per hour, the driver of the car in front of me inexplicably abruptly slowed down and turned left into a driveway, right in the path of an oncoming car. The second car hit the first car squarely on the passenger side door causing one to end up in the ditch and the other ended up perpendicular to the road in the middle of the southbound lane.

Well, because I was right there and I do have experience responding to traffic accidents as a law enforcement officer, I pulled over as Kordan told me she was calling 911. I then sprinted to the scene of the accident, which was about 100 feet behind my vehicle, which was now parked on the side of the road half in a snowbank. I rushed to the vehicles and checked on the sole occupants of each. Both were lucid and there were no visible signs of trauma. Both drivers claimed to be "OK" and commenced calling loved ones.

I left them in their vehicles and turned my attention to the highway on which I was standing. Although it had been less than two minutes since the crash occurred, traffic was already backed up over a quarter-mile in each direction, so I took it upon myself to take control of the situation. For the next 15 minutes, I directed traffic around the crash victim who was still in her car in the middle of the road. Eventually, three single-person patrols arrived on the scene. From my vantage point on the road, I observed them initially clustered around the first one, and then the other victim of the crash.

During this time I was observing the responding officers, I saw one person taking notes and the other two standing beside him with their hands in the pockets of their parkas. Here is where the judging comes in. I was getting irritated as I watched three officers do the work of one, while I was doing their job about 100 feet away. So, I hollered over to one of them and told him to come over to me. He did.

As I continued to direct traffic on the highway around the crashed vehicle and now two people standing in the middle of the road (the cop and me), I asked him if he thought he or the other guy could maybe stop what they were doing and take traffic control off my hands so that I could get going. He told me "No, they'll figure it out." I was incredulous so I asked him to clarify, because I must have misunderstood him. I said, "Do you think these truck drivers, bus drivers, moms and dads taking kids to school, and kids driving themselves can figure out how to traverse this area with a car in the middle of the road and an ambulance arriving soon?" He told me yes and released me from the scene. I left. I then sat in my vehicle for a moment and observed the actions of the three officers. The same one who had been taking notes upon his arrival at the scene continued to do so and the other two stood on the side of the road talking to one another. I pulled away shaking my head.

The moral of the story is that I had observed what I thought was less than appropriate behavior by the three officers within the first few moments after their arrival on the scene. One was working while two watched. I did not think very highly of them and my assessment was reinforced when I was summarily dismissed from the scene by an observing officer who wanted to let drivers "figure it out." I was appalled. Their deportment caused me to pass initial judgment and their continued behavior proved me right. They were never going to get the respect from me their positions warranted.

When I entered adulthood, the concept of "role models" was not one I considered. I did not look at others and consciously think "they are a positive role model," just like I didn't consider it my job to be one. Well, being conscious of the responsibility as a role model changed when I had kids and was further reinforced once I started teaching.

Back in 1999, my wife became pregnant. Like all conscientious women who are expecting, she opted to quit consuming alcohol. It had been my plan all along to stop consuming alcohol when she became pregnant because it would have not felt right for me to continue to party and consume alcohol when she could not because of her responsibility to our unborn child.

Now, I would like to tell you that I quit immediately: I did not. We found out she was pregnant on February 12, 1999, a Friday. Well, it just so happened that we had plans for the following evening to attend a concert at a nearby casino and one of the members of the band worked with Kori. So, I opted to stop consuming alcohol after one last hoorah. Let me tell you, I went out in style! I consumed my last alcoholic beverage during the wee hours of February 14 and my hangover went away on February 16. For the ensuing months, I did not consume any alcohol. We ended up losing that baby and then Kori got pregnant a couple of months later and I did not consume any alcohol during that time.

In May 2000, our daughter was born. I could have started to consume alcohol again, but I knew that I was getting up at zero dark thirty the following morning regardless of what I consumed each night and I did not want to deal with the after-effects of alcohol with a newborn. Fast forward a year and I landed my first teaching job. I still did not consume alcohol and I do not recall consciously thinking about being a positive role model for my kids or for those I taught.

In that first job, I taught 9th graders and I loved interacting with them. At the end of every class on Fridays, I would always encourage them to practice safe behavior over the weekend. I would also throw in something like "don't drink and swim!" because "don't drink and drive" didn't make sense for 14 and 15-year-olds. One day a kid yelled back to me as he was leaving the room "You don't drink and swim either, Mr. Kopp!" I yelled to him that I didn't drink. He spun around and came back into the room and in front of another 15+ kids, asked me what I meant. I reiterated that I did not drink alcohol at all, let alone when I was swimming. He, along with several other kids, was incredulous. I could see the look of awe on their faces when they realized an adult in their lives did not consume alcohol. It seemed to be a foreign concept to them.

That did it for me. I realized that I needed to be a role model for all the kids in every school in which I worked and for my kids. I do not think ill of others who consume alcohol (Kori will drink about a case of beer a year), I simply wanted to provide all the kids in my life an example of someone who does not drink, but still enjoys life. All of us can be role models that fit our lifestyles. This just happens to be the method I chose. I am now 23 years into that commitment and do not regret the decision.

"Professionalism" is a good way to consider the concept of being beyond reproach. Professionalism can be somewhat of an ambiguous term, but I think most people would somehow define it through the lens of appropriate behavior: in other words, being beyond reproach.

The lack of professionalism rankled me and others with whom I was stationed in the 109th in Frankfurt. As I mentioned earlier, we were the "Palace Guards" and were in charge of security for the V Corps Headquarters complex in Frankfurt. As you probably assumed, there were a whole lot of higher-ranking people associated with a corps' headquarters. So, daily we encountered high-ranking people and occasional VIPs that were of even higher rank, both civilian and military. Regrettably, what sometimes comes with people of high rank is the air of superiority. This oftentimes manifests itself when people of high rank and/or position interact with those they consider "beneath their station".

This was frequently the case in Frankfurt and the poor treatment my fellow military police officers and I encountered daily was addressed by our platoon sergeant, Sergeant First Class (SFC) Keene (his first name escapes me). Well, SFC Keene tried to bring some levity to the situation because he told us some of the people we encountered daily had degrees in asshology and they were trained to be asshologists. He went on to explain how it was required of their training to be asshologists every time they interacted with us.

After interactions with asshologists, we found ourselves shaking our heads at the degree holder as they were departing our location. We even went so far as to compare asshology stories at the end of the day over a few beverages. Needless to say, these asshologists did not understand the idea of having deportment beyond reproach. SFC Keene did not rid the world of asshologists, but he sure made it a lot more entertaining for us when we had to deal with them.

I have been lauded for my willpower over the years whether it is regarding alcohol, avoiding foods I shouldn't eat, or never wavering from my convictions. I think the willpower I have allows me to do what I think is right. I approached all the positions I have held with the intent of making the most of them.

When I was in the army I kept my head down and did my job. This allowed me to be on the fast track to promotion. Once I established my credibility in Panamá I was chosen to be the military police station desk sergeant. I parlayed that experience into being the non-commissioned officer in charge (NCOIC) of S-1, Personnel, and S-4, Logistics at the brigade level for the Military Police Command in Panamá. It was while I was serving in that role that I acknowledged my wanderlust and decided to opt into civilian life, despite the fast track my career was on.

Once I started in education, my career progressed quickly as well. I only taught for five years and then was an associate principal and principal for another five before I became a district administrator. There are others whose careers in education have mirrored mine, but I can tell you, that acting in a manner that is beyond reproach helped my career advancement in the military and public education. Now that I own my own consulting companies, I know my leadership tenets have drawn clients to our business.

Being beyond reproach can help you in all facets of your life and will help you become a better leader and a better person.

BE THE BUFFALO

I mentioned earlier how my tenets may not have a rank order of importance and their appearance in this book are by no means indicative of the relative importance of one versus another. Having said that, I think Being the Buffalo may be my favorite characteristic and the one for which I am best known. Incidentally, "Be the Buffalo" is tattooed on my right forearm and it happens to be my favorite tattoo of the nine that I have. Additionally, I mentor, coach, and consult with other leaders through my second company, Leading Like a Buffalo, Inc.

Being the buffalo is an approach to life that helps you get confrontation behind you.

I have always lived my adult life based on this tenet but did not have a name for it until about 12-13 years ago when I was reading a magazine. I happened to be downstairs waiting for Kori so we could leave and I had about two minutes to kill. So, I picked up Kori's most recent copy of Oprah's magazine and flipped through it. I am not a "read a magazine article" type of guy, but I am a "look at charts and lists" type of guy. As I was skimming through the magazine the caption on a small list caught my attention "The Top 10 Things I Have Learned in Life," and it was authored by political strategist Donna Brazile. I read the list and the only one that I recall is "Be the Buffalo," because it resonated and spoke to me. It allowed me to figure out who I was at my core.

I have taught the concept of being the buffalo countless times to high school students in leadership classes, my coworkers, and my contemporaries. This is what it means: when you are on the United States' Great Plains you can see for what seems like forever! With this vast line of sight comes the ability to see storms that are coming your way. The two genders of the American Bison, a traditional inhabitant of the Great Plains, have opposite reactions to the approach of the storms: the females, also known as the cows, turn tail and run upon seeing a storm approaching. The males, also known as the buffalo, charge through the storm to get through it faster.

So, how does a buffalo charging through a storm equate to a leadership tenet? Well, I would argue it is about more than just leadership and could be how one lives his/her life. You see, the storm simply represents a problem. Consider any problem, big or small, that you had to address with another person. This other person could be a co-worker, a boss, a friend, a relative...you get the idea. Now consider the angst you felt before having interaction with that other person and compare it to the angst you felt during the interaction. For most people, most of the time, the anxiety that is experienced before addressing the problem with another is worse than the actual discussion itself. This is a prime example of being the buffalo.

I can say that I am not sure where I learned to be the buffalo. Back in 1999 my maternal grandmother was in a nursing home and was on the precipice of death. Kori and I went to visit her and encountered several of my cousins in Bird's room. Yes, we called her Bird, despite her given name being Emma and the fact that she was my grandmother. Anyway, Bird had a seizure while we were there and my cousins looked at me and one of them stated that everything was going to be ok because I was there. I was taken aback because I did not realize people in my family viewed me in that light. I had not had a lot of interaction with those particular cousins as an adult, so their impression of me must have come from when we were kids.

I think I first learned the importance of being the buffalo when I was a military police officer. As I described earlier, I had to be dispatched to domestic disturbances at the various duty stations at which I served around the world. Being dispatched to domestic situations always brought with it a sense of dread: I knew I was about to invade someone's home where tensions were already high. Because of this, I had to control the situation the second I encountered people, whether it was in the yard or as I was walking into their homes. If I did not control the situation someone may have been in danger of getting hurt and that someone may have been me! So, I controlled it and despite the many times I removed people from homes, no one ever got hurt while I was present.

Another situation occurred while I was a military police officer that brought being the buffalo to my conscious thought, despite not having the name for it yet. Back on October 30, 1991, I was working as a night shift patrol supervisor at Fort Devens, MA. About a dozen of us went to work that night as vehicle patrols and gate guards for the entirety of Fort Devens and we expected bad things because of a storm that had been developing off the coast of Gloucester, MA. At the time there was no official name for that storm, but it has subsequently been called The Perfect Storm and its existence is well chronicled in many books and a movie by the same name.

As we took to the road that night at 2200hrs (10 pm), winds were high and landfall by the storm had occurred. By that time in my life, I had never been in a hurricane, and after that night, I decided I never wanted to live where there was a possibility for such in the future!

Early on in the shift, the weather became more intense as the front rapidly swept through the area bringing with it strong winds that ended up knocking down a lot of trees, and with the trees went the power to the fort. Sometime between 2300 and 2400hrs the wind had subsided and I was dispatched to the parade grounds (a large, grassy area) that was behind 8-10 barracks, each of which was home to 100-150 soldiers. The radio/telephone operator (aka dispatcher) told me the residents of the barracks had vacated their rooms and had congregated on the parade grounds and the crowd was becoming agitated.

I happened to be the first one on the scene and my backup, a K-9 patrol, was about five minutes out. I had two choices: wait for backup and chance someone getting hurt or take control of the situation in an attempt to quell this escalating agitation. I opted to be the buffalo and waded into the mass of 1,000+ soldiers who were cloaked in darkness. On my hips, I had a military police nightstick and a Beretta 9mm pistol. In my right hand, I carried a 3-D Cell Maglite and I was alone.

Despite all of us being soldiers in the United States Army, my presence was not well-received. There was a lot of heckling and a bit of jostling as I made my way through the crowd to the center where several people were squaring up. I immediately took control of the situation by ordering the people to stand down, disperse, and return to their respective barracks. After a few tense moments and a few taunts from the tightly clustered crowd, soldiers near the center started to turn away and encouraged others to do so. Within a few minutes, the crowd was gone leaving behind small clusters of soldiers near several of the barracks. I then made my way back to the parking lot and debriefed the K-9 handler who had arrived as the crowd was dispersing.

Being the buffalo has its place in all parts of our working society including public education. When I served as a leader in various districts I had numerous conversations with other leaders about being the buffalo. The concept was always well-received and eye-opening to some. As is my tendency, I repeatedly coached my teammates and got them to realize being the buffalo is very beneficial.

In one of the districts, I had a teammate who had a dicey relationship with one of the teachers in the district. This relationship caused disgruntlement on both the teacher's part and my fellow administrator's part. I witnessed this for three years and had discussions with the other administrator about being the buffalo.

Because personal, negative interactions are not fun, this other administrator did not embrace my encouragement and lashed out at me by accusing me of "liking confrontation!" I tried to explain to this administrator that I did not like it, but rather liked it behind me more than I liked it in front of me.

Four years into our working relationship I found myself once again coaching this administrator and attempting to get her to understand the importance of being the buffalo. For whatever reason, this time she accepted the fact that she needed to talk to the teacher. I distinctly remember when she got to that point: as she was sitting across from me at my desk, she leaned forward, pounded both her fists on the desk, and roared "I'm going to be the buffalo!" She then stormed out of my office with a purposeful gait.

I made the assumption she would come back to my office within the hour and report to me about the outcome of her meeting. Surprisingly, it only took her 15 minutes to return to my office and she had a pep in her step. She had talked to the teacher and they realized there had been some misunderstandings on both sides from their initial encounter and they talked it all out and were now good. I reinforced what she had done by making her focus on the fact that she had worried about this relationship and issue for 3+ years and she fixed it in 15 minutes. Being the buffalo in action.

Two other teammates I have had over the years embraced being the buffalo immediately. One of them is Lynn Bub, an educational leader who personifies "Being the Buffalo" and brings it to life daily. When she encounters issues she addresses them promptly. I always channel her skill in doing this when I am faced with a particularly tough situation that I have to address. I think "Lynn would be the buffalo right now, so I must as well." She is one of my motivators.

Another one of my former teammates was Mike Juech, who has been previously mentioned in this book. One time we were discussing something that occurred in the district in which he was working. He told me the background of an issue and then stated "I then pulled a Dan Kopp on them." I had to ask, "what the @#$% does that mean?" He went on to explain to me that he was the buffalo and that he took control of a situation just like I am prone to do. The issue in question was resolved and he and his coworkers moved on from it.

Being the buffalo can be problematic if you have a desire to act, but do not know what to do. When this occurs you must check yourself and figure out the right approach before taking action. This entails getting all the facts, plus affords you the time needed to regain your composure.

Several years ago I witnessed an interaction between two administrators with whom I worked. To put it mildly, I was less than happy about what I had witnessed. I wanted to address it immediately, but not only did I not know what to say or do, I was also irate. I knew I needed to assess the situation, figure out a solution, and let my ire subside. I then slept on it, or as most leaders can relate: tossed and turned all night thinking about it.

By the next morning, I had my emotions in check and had settled on an approach to take with the other leaders. I subsequently addressed the issue with each of them individually and coached them into realizing how to fix the issue. That night I received calls from each of the other administrators and both of them were very upbeat about the discussion the two of them had just had and both stated the issue was behind them. I don't remember what the issue was or what I said to them. I only remember the lesson that I had reinforced for myself: take time to control your emotions and learn all of the facts before being the buffalo.

At the inception of one of my jobs, I had to be the buffalo with the board of education at the very first meeting! During the regular, routine part of the meeting, one of the board members asked a question about something that was not in his purview. A little background: a board's job is to write policies. One of those policies delegated operational control of the district to me: it was a standard policy that most, if not all boards of education across the country have.

The question was about something that was my job, rather than the board's job. Once we got into a closed session, another board member asked me a question about an applicant we had for an open position, which was also not her job. I had to address both questions to establish the right relationship with the members of the board. So, I asked them to allow me to speak for a few moments because I had to address some things.

They allowed me to do so and I reminded them that we had discussed trust during the interview process. I further explained that I had not earned their trust yet (I had only been in the district for about 10 days), but they needed to start trusting me and let me do my job. I went further by pointing out that the individual board members were out of line by asking those two questions. One of the members of the board, who happened to be one of the offending parties, crossed her arms and gave me a sly smile.

I went to work the next morning expecting one of two

things: 1) I was going to be talked to by the board president about me overstepping my bounds, or 2) I was going to get a positive email from the guilty board member who had crossed her arms the night before. I received the email and gratitude was expressed by the board member for putting the board members in their place because from her point of view, they had been overstepping their bounds for years and they needed to be set straight. She then told me to go out and do the job she knew I could do. Well, that worked out well!

This interaction with my board, along with various others, led another district administrator to say to me "You are a better leader than I because you handle things more forcefully." This sounded harsh, but I knew his intent did not match his words, so we talked about being the buffalo. Once I explained to him how I liked getting confrontation behind me, he realized that I simply handled things in a more timely manner than he did, rather than handling them more forcefully. He tended to let things stew and get out of hand a little bit before addressing them and he thought his approach exuded weakness. We discussed it long enough for him to understand my approach was about timeliness, rather than force. We have spoken a lot since and he is still a work in progress as he tries fully to embrace being the buffalo.

If you are not adept at being the buffalo, embracing this tenet may be challenging because it is "not you." I want you to consider that a moment. I am not suggesting you change how you handle a situation. I am merely suggesting that you handle it in a more timely manner so that you can get it behind you. Leaders, I implore you, BE THE BUFFALO!

CONCLUSION

As you can see, the leadership tenets that drive me are vast and varied. I usually am not consciously thinking about them when I act. However, I recently started journaling which reaffirmed that these tenets are alive and well within me.

My partner Mike, who has been mentioned several other times in this book, and I had a conversation about leadership not too long ago. Before that discussion, the two main things we were working on with our clients seemed unrelated. At times we were mentoring and coaching other leaders and other times we were working with employers and helping them save time and money while they attract and retain great people.

Unrelated, yes?

No.

During that discussion on leadership, we discussed how everyone has a powerful uniqueness. It does not matter if we are interacting with a mentee about his/her skills or with an employer when we are focused on the great things employees do. Each time we are talking about "The Power of Me." For leaders, it is easy to visualize: each of us has values and skills that allow us to be good leaders. Employers can identify the greatness within each of their employees and compensate them according. In essence, they identify The Power of Me in each individual.

When I started drafting this book my intent was not to give you a step-by-step approach to leadership. Rather, I had intended to show you who I was, why I did the things I did, and how they worked for me. Now that I have spent months delving into my mind I realize the leadership tenets in this book can and should be embraced by all leaders. As I have explained, you cannot do things as I do and I cannot do things as you do. However, everyone has it in them to embrace the tenets I have laid out and make them their own. I don't profess to know what actions you can perform that will speak louder than your words in your current role, but I can challenge you to close your mouth and start acting. Others will notice.

Focus within.
Focus on the strengths you have.
Identify your values.
Determine why those values are important to you.
Become a better version of yourself by focusing on
THE POWER OF ME.

You can do this.
Good luck.